KEYSTONES

MAKE DISCIPLES

Vol. 2: Acts Through Philemon

By George Grant

Standfast Books

Standfast Books
Franklin, Tennessee

To My Beloved Covenant Community:
Parish Presbyterian Church

CONTENTS

1

FOREWORD: DAWN AT KILMANY

On September 3, 1805, Thomas Chalmers, a minister in the Church of Scotland, confided to his brother that the "clergyman's life" was a "dull and unvaried course [offering] little new or interesting." In the same year he vented that a clergyman is "one of those ill-fated beings whom the malignant touch of ordination has condemned to a life of ignorance and obscurity; a being who must bid adieu, it seems, to every flattering anticipation, and drivel out the remainder of his days in insignificance." Such words may seem strange indeed, coming from an ordained minister in the Kirk of John Knox, the very cradle of Presbyterianism. But all this was about to change, as Chalmers soon experienced a radical, evangelical conversion. He eventually became not only a highly acclaimed, spellbinding preacher, but a visionary and energetic churchman as well, taking the helm of the Church of Scotland and, through the Disruption of 1843, that of the Free Church of Scotland.

Sadly, Chalmers' derogatory sentiments about the ministry above were not at all unheard of; they breathed what many deemed the chilling spirit of Moderatism, the dominant religious mindset of 18th century Scotland. In the name of reason and humanism, Moderates generally downplayed and at least implicitly negated the old evangelical doctrines of the fallenness of man, predestination, the substitutionary work of Christ, and the new birth. Deriding evangelical spirituality as fanaticism, they tended to preach morality and civility, deed over creed, and espoused a much more synergistic view of salvation. Contrasted with the more evangelically-minded "orthodox" or the "Popular" party of the 18th century, such as Witherspoon and Willison, at the time of Chalmers' entrance into the ministry, the pro-Enlightenment Moderates held sway in the state Church.

During this time, it was not uncommon for a Moderate-minded young man to seek the holy ministry for reasons other than the 'cure of souls.' Because of its endowment, a parish charge could become a sinecure, furnishing its incumbent with ample leisure time to devote to whatever literary or scientific pursuit he might have. As a man of his time, Chalmers followed suit. His real passion was not ministry but mathematics. So when he received the presentation to the rural Fifeshire parish of Kilmany, he enthusiastically accepted it on two counts—it secured him a generous stipend, and it happened to be close to St. Andrews, the home of the oldest of Scotland's prestigious universities. On May 12, 1803, then, the Presbytery of Cupar ordained and inducted him into his charge. To be sure, the new pastor prepared his homilies and made occasional rounds. But he threw himself into his favorite avocation by conducting a course in mathematics in the university community, with the ambition of securing a professorship.

But this move was not without criticism. His own presbytery accused him of compromising his spiritual charge in the interest of secular pursuits and ordered him either to desist from the classes or receive ecclesiastical censure. Because of his non-clerical ambitions, he had grossly neglected household visitations, catechizing the youth, and other pastoral responsibilities. While technically Chalmers was not yet a 'pluralist'—a minister holding both the offices of pastor and professor while collecting livings from both—he was certainly a functional one. And though he returned to Kilmany on Sundays, he was often away; during his maiden year he was very arguably a 'non-resident' pastor, residing in St. Andrews Monday through Saturday. And, not surprisingly, he prepared his sermons hastily. But Chalmers would have none of it. Indignant, he could testify from experience that "after the satisfactory discharge of his parish duties, a minister may enjoy five days in the week of uninterrupted leisure, for the prosecution of any science in which his taste may dispose him to engage."

Thus, one searches in vain in his Moderate phase to find even the smallest embryo of his future interest in parish ministry. At that point, it was but a stepping-stone to academic advancement. He felt no burden for his parish, much less had it captured his imagination as a catalyst for the rebirth of his beloved Scotland. And the reason was close at hand, since in his later judgment he had not been reborn. Now, Chalmers certainly was cognizant of the legacy and responsibility of the Kirk's parish ministry—painfully so. Not only did he experience pushback from his ecclesiastical peers, but his own father was a constant reminder. John Chalmers, a pious son of the Kirk, was concerned if not unnerved about his son's situation and the ramifications it would have on the spiritual well-being of his parish. Knowing his father's "scruples about clerical residence," Chalmers reassured: "Even at present I am able to devote as much time and as much attention to other subjects, as I will be under the necessity of doing next winter, and after all I discharge my duties, I hope, in a satisfactory manner. With regard to non-residence, that is only to last for six months." But on another occasion, he bristled with self-justification:

I beg you will not distress yourself by any suspicions as to my indifference to the parochial duties. From the infinite variety of men's dispositions, there must be different methods of expressing the feelings of their hearts; and they will employ different instruments for improving the purity of their purposes. I feel that the solitude of a few days would be to me a painful and unmeaning solemnity. Accuse me of indifference when you have observed me deficient in any of the essential duties — when you have observed me shrinking from any of those labours which the cares of a parish impose.

Far from showing signs of budging by the appeals of his devout father, Chalmers stubbornly doubled down.

Then came the change. During a season of debilitating illness from mid-1809 into 1810, Chalmers sensed that he was nearing the boundaries of eternity. In February 1810, he confided to a fellow minister from his sickbed,

My confinement has fixed on my heart a very strong impression of the insignificance of time — an impression which I trust will not abandon me though I again reach the heyday of health and vigour. This should be the first step to another impression still more salutary — the magnitude of eternity. Strip human life of its connexion with a higher scene of existence, and it is the illusion of an instant, an unmeaning farce, a series of visions and projects, and convulsive efforts, which terminate in nothing.

Evangelical authors but recently spurned were revisited and read with increasing interest. Chief among these was William Wilberforce, whose *Practical View* winsomely compelled Chalmers to reconsider the evangelical message and its "peculiar doctrines" he had before nauseated. Other social, political, and personal factors were doubtless at play. But as a distinctly religious conversion, it was, as Chalmers' modern biographer put it, "inexplicable. Something undoubtedly happened to him between 1809 and 1811, which fundamentally changed the way he conceived of God and the world, so that he committed himself to the Evangelical movement which once he had despised."

After recovering from the illness, he returned to the pulpit a changed man. His people immediately sensed that there had been a revolution in the mind of their pastor, as he preached with a newfound unction and immediacy.

"He would bend over the pulpit," said one of his old hearers, "and press us to take the gift, as if he held it that moment in his hand, and would not be satisfied till every one of us had got possession of it. And often when the sermon was over, and the psalm was sung, and he rose to pronounce the blessing, he would break out afresh with some new entreaty, unwilling to let us go until he had made one more effort to persuade us to accept of it."

Word spread to nearby villages of the "new miracle of Divine grace," and services swelled with interested worshipers. Before long, the new convert was soon converting others. On one Sabbath in 1812 after Chalmers had preached on John 3:16, two sons of the parish, Alexander Paterson and Robert Edie, met as the congregation dispersed. Upon finding themselves alone, Alexander asked Robert whether he had "felt anything particularly" that morning, confiding "I never felt myself to be a lost sinner till to-day, when I was listening to that sermon." Robert rejoined, "It is very strange … it was just the same with me."

Strangely enough, Chalmers' aspect and pulpit manner were unimpressive, further encumbered by his habit of his word-for-word reading of full manuscripts. The palpable electricity, then, could mystify and defy explanation. Stewart Brown† suggests that Chalmers' new, deeply held doctrinal convictions, his appeal to the imaginative and emotive romantic spirit of the age, and at the same time his synthesis of that new romanticism with an older Scottish enlightenment style, forcefully combined to impact his audiences. Chalmers, however, directly ascribed this to a hidden spring in 'the secret place of the Most High.' He had by the regenerating power of the Spirit's work rediscovered the Bible as God's written Word, counting it as heavenly manna for his newfound spiritual appetite. William Hanna* records the following illustrative anecdote:

His regular and earnest study of the Bible was one of the first and most noticeable effects of Mr. Chalmers' conversion. His nearest neighbour and most frequent visitor was old John Bonthron, who, having once seen better days, was admitted to an easy and privileged familiarity, in the exercise of which one day before the memorable illness, he said to Mr. Chalmers—"I find you aye busy, sir, with one thing or another, but come when I may, I never find you at your studies for the Sabbath." "Oh an hour or two on the Saturday evening is quite enough for that," was the minister's answer. But now the change had come, and John, on entering the manse, often found Mr. Chalmers poring eagerly over the pages of the Bible. The difference was too striking to escape notice, and with the freedom given him, which he was ready enough to use, he said, "I never come in now, sir, but I find you aye at your Bible." "All too little, John, all too little," was the significant reply.

The new pastor no longer read his Bible simply as a professional obligation, gleaning bits and pieces to adorn his moralizing homilies. For him it was an intensely personal and transformative exercise. In particular, he was borne by the mighty current running through its pages: the Gospel remedy— Christ crucified—fully and freely offered to helpless sinners and received by faith alone. Before, he preached morality, a dry well set before the thirsty. Now, having himself found the Living Water, he summoned others and, surprisingly, found moral transformation as its byproduct.

Further, just as Kilmany's pulpit changed, so also did Kilmany's parish. In the final three years of Chalmers' pastoral labors in Kilmany, he left off numbers in the abstract to devote his attention to more concrete ones—his parishioners. They were the same people as before, living in the same geographically-defined charge assigned him by his presbytery. But they were now his flock, head-for-head, rich and poor, saints and sinners. Each of them had immortal souls, destined for eternity. So what before could be done in less than a weekend now took on more than full-time proportions. In 1811, he wrote in his journal:

Now that I have got well, let me devote a great part of my time to the business of my parish; and may it be the main anxiety of my life, Lord, to promote Thy glory, and to testify the gratitude of my heart for the merciful scheme of reconciliation made known and offered to us in the gospel. May I every day feel a growing interest in the covenant of grace; and let me evince in my own conduct that the doctrine of faith is a doctrine according to godliness.

This new resolve yielded a thorough-going regimen of preaching and pastoring, embodying the old ideal of the Presbyterian man of God. Not only did he prepare for and enter the 'sacred desk' with fresh unction on the Sabbaths, but he energetically labored between them within his "home-walk." Every house was his, and he visited every family dutifully each year if not more. In this experience, he was gradually rediscovering his ancestral inheritance—the Scottish parish ministry.

In 1813 and 1814, Chalmers made ample personal records of his visits throughout the parish. Together with his private journal entries, his memoranda entitled "Records of spiritual intercourse with my people" give a glimpse of his intensifying enthusiasm for pastoral ministry. In his rounds, he would visit with the families in their own homes, read Scripture, give lively exhortation from the text to the hearts of the family, and pray with and for them. But further, he took care to engage in practical diagnostics, looking for disciplines of spiritual health the Kirk had standardized during the Reformation and post-Reformation periods and modeled by eminent ministers well into the 18th century. Chief among these was whether the family members were all in regular attendance on the public means of grace. It is to be kept in mind that not all parishioners were communicants, that is, individuals eligible for communion by a public profession of faith. The index of this profession was a working knowledge of basic Christian doctrine and a life free from gross or 'scandalous' sins. Yet all parishioners, eligible or not, were at least obliged to sit under the preaching. For, as the Westminster Shorter Catechism put it, "The reading, but especially the preaching of the Word, is an effectual means of convincing and converting sinners, and of building them up in holiness and comfort, through faith unto salvation." So the prime diagnostic was whether such an individual or household was in regular attendance on the Sabbath services. Naturally, then, we read such notes in Chalmers' personal records as, "Mr D [sic] absenting himself from all ordinances."

Then there was the second main diagnostic, family worship. This was a simple, yet time-honored Scottish evangelical practice in which heads of households would call all members of the family together for a kind of short, domestic worship service. The Bible would be read, a metrical psalm sung, children and servants would be drilled in their ability to recite and comprehend the Shorter Catechism, and the father would lead all to the throne of grace. The national Kirk had long obliged pastors and their elders to ensure that their parishioners, communicant or otherwise, were dutifully conducting daily family worship. Consequently, we see Chalmers urging this practice throughout his efforts. "Had a day at Mr Edies. . . . I thought the Edies little impressed with my exhortation about family religion, and the care of watching over the souls of children." "[May] 6. . . . Mr. Keyden arrived in the evening. Have not yet succeeded in prevailing on [him] to have family worship." But the good pastor was undeterred, as four days later he writes, "Sunday [May] 10. . . . Had some earnest and particular conversation with Mr. Keyden in the hearing of Miss King his housekeeper, and prevailed upon him to have family worship in the evening." And just for good measure, two days later, we read, "Got family worship performed again at Mr. Keyden's, and am delighted to hear him say, that he intends to continue the system."

Above all, though, his visits were errands in the interests of eternity. Beyond ensuring the routines of spiritual maintenance and growth were in place, the pastor wanted to know how it fared with each one's soul. "March 23. Opened myself more freely to Mr. B. He acquiesces. You carry his assent always along with you, but you feel as if you have no point of resistance and are making no impression." Continually transcending trivialities, he would sometimes risk touching a raw nerve in the service of souls. "June 2. Mr Miller . . . sent for me in prospect of death. A man of profligate and profane habits, and who resents my calling him an unworthy sinner." "[June] 4. Visited again Mr. Miller. Found him worse but displeased at my method of administering to his spiritual wants; said that it was most unfortunate he had sent for me. . . . seemed quite determined to wrap himself in an Antinomian security." And sincere communicants, already judged the 'well,' yet stood in need of routine checkups. Such "examinations" were usually coordinated with Communion seasons: "[August] 8. Reexamined a great many communicants—and I pray God for the origin and progress of religion in their souls. O fit me for the great charge of guiding them to the way of peace."

The following anecdote is recounted by one of the members of his Kilmany parish, Mr. Robert Edie, offering a vignette into how Chalmers went about his family visits and how he earnestly sought to win souls under each roof:

I have a very lively recollection of the intense earnestness of his addresses on occasions of visitation in my father's house, when he would unconsciously move forward on his chair to the very margin of it, in his anxiety to impart to the family and servants the impressions of eternal things that so filled his own soul. "It would take a great book," said he, beginning his address to one of these household congregations, "to contain the names of all the individuals that have ever lived, from the days of Adam down to the present hour; but there is one name that takes in the whole of them—that name is sinner: and here is a message from God to every one that bears that name—'The blood of Jesus Christ, His Son, cleanseth us from all sin.'"

Edie then gives another anecdote demonstrating keen pastoral insight:

Wishing to tell them what kind of faith God would have them to cherish, and what kind of fear, and how it was that instead of hindering each other, the right fear and the right faith worked into each others' hands, he said, "It is just as if you threw out a rope to a drowning man. Faith is the hold he takes of it. It is fear which makes him grasp it with all his might; and the greater his fear, the firmer his hold."

Not content with hoarding his newly discovered riches, Chalmers lavished them on his fellow bankrupts.

Combined with this house-to-house program of visitation, he frequently catechized his parish. The Reformation fathers had devised this practice of dialogic instruction especially with a view to preparing and admitting all who would partake of the Lord's Supper, lest the Table be profaned by the ignorant or otherwise unworthy. Having divided his parish into several districts, he would assemble the inhabitants in some convenient location such as a barn and ask young and old, male and female, to repeat and explain the catechism's answers. By his queries, he ascertained to what degree they grasped what they had learned by rote. But this catechist was no drill sergeant. Throughout each exercise, he was preeminently pastoral, often showing delicacy so as not to embarrass anyone unnecessarily. He might, for example, ask a general question on a certain point. If no soul was brave enough to venture an answer, he would take all the blame to himself for not having asked the question clearly enough to be understood and proceeded to make another go of it.

Last, as adjuncts to his spiritual office, he involved himself in the oversight of the parish schools and local poor relief. Both of these responsibilities had also been handed down to him by law and custom; and while ministers were primarily carers of the soul, their prominent position the yet religiously integrated society of rural Scotland entailed a measure of their clerical involvement. Brown summarizes the Kirk's outlook, "In its ideal, the parish ministry focused upon fulfilling the needs of the whole 'natural' man—intellectual, moral, and physical—as well as upon providing vehicles of divine grace for the salvation of God's elect saints." Chalmers clearly embraced this more holistic approach to ministry and endeavored to implement it among the degraded poor of his future city missions.

Given this radical revolution in pastoral ministry, it is hardly surprising that his earlier career in Moderatism became a matter of profound self-reproach. He had omitted the 'one thing needful,' a sin fearfully aggravated by his position as an ordained caretaker of souls. On September 7, 1812, Chalmers wrote in his journal, "I again prayed for the forgiveness of my long continued neglect and indolence as a Christian minister." Two months later we read, "Prayed for the repentance and remission of my sin of negligence in holy things as a minister of the gospel—for my parish and for the more attentive and conscientious discharge of my engagements amongst them."

His penitence eventually went public. While it is true that Chalmers' conversion in or around 1811 did not produce an immediate, open disavowal of his early career, it was clear to all that "he now preached the faith which he once destroyed." Many years later, however, he did go on record. During a debate in the General Assembly of 1825 on the subject of pluralities—against which Chalmers spoke with eloquence—an unexpected challenge put him on his heels. One of his Moderate opponents spoke and read from a pamphlet of his published back in 1805, when he infamously declared that he could devote a mere two days of the week to his parish duties, freeing him to pursue whatever avocations might please him the other five. At this, Chalmers arose—yet not to defend but to incriminate himself:

Verily I believed that my unfortunate pamphlet had long ere now descended into the tomb of merited oblivion, and that there it was mouldering in silence, forgotten and disregarded. But since that gentleman has brought it forward in the face of this house, I can assure him that I feel grateful to him from the bottom of my heart, for the opportunity he has now afforded me of making a public recantation of the sentiments it contains. . . . I now confess myself to have been guilty of a heinous crime, and I now stand a repentant culprit before the bar of this venerable assembly. . . .

I was at that time, Sir, more devoted to mathematics than to the literature of my profession; and feeling grieved and indignant at what I conceived an undue reflection on the abilities and education of our clergy, I came

*forward with that pamphlet to rescue them from what I deemed an un-
merited reproach, by maintaining that a devoted and exclusive attention
to the study of mathematics was not dissonant to the proper habits of
a clergyman. Alas! Sir, so I thought in my ignorance and pride. I have
now no reserve in saying that the sentiment was wrong, and that, in the
utterance of it, I penned what was most outrageously wrong. Strangely
blinded that I was! What, Sir, is the object of mathematical science?
Magnitude and the proportions of magnitude. But then, Sir, I had
forgotten two magnitudes—I thought not of the littleness of time—I
recklessly thought not of the greatness of eternity.*

Not surprisingly, his evangelical ministry in this sleepy rural
village did not go unnoticed, and all the more as this pen-
itent proselyte was a dynamic preacher. So it was that in
1815, he was called to and accepted one of the most import-
ant charges in Scotland, the Tron Kirk in Glasgow. It was
there that Chalmers began to launch his program of parish
experiments, seeking to reverse the spiritual and moral blight
of Scotland's teeming cities.

From Kilmany to his final experiment in the slums of Edinburgh, Chalmers was preeminently a man of the Word. By
the secret working of the Spirit, it had proved itself the un-
tamable, all-conquering power of God. It had mastered him,
impelling him to dedicate the rest of his life to extend the
Bible's gracious reign over Scotland and the world. He sus-

tained that energy in the closet, with his Bible and his God. These volumes are issued in this spirit. Read, probe, ponder, and be changed "from glory to glory, even as by the Spirit of the Lord." Then rise, and go forth as Jesus' witnesses into a world insensibly starving for Jesus, the "Word made flesh."

Rev. Michael J. Ives
Presbyterian Reformed Church of R.I.

---

* William Hanna, son-in-law and official biographer of Chalmers

† Stewart Brown, author of "Thomas Chalmers and the Godly Commonwealth in Scotland"

2
RECOVERING THE OLD PATHS

"The Spirit guides us unto all truth and all truth is to be found in the Bible; the Spirit therefore guides us unto the Bible."

Thomas Chalmers

"We have to make the Bible our Vade Mecum: our book of reference, our book of trust. Let us be convinced more and more of the prodigious fertility of the Bible. How much lies hidden and unobserved, even after many perusals; and surely if it be true that a man may read it an hundred times and find something on his next reading which he missed on all his former ones, oftener recourse to this means of grace bids fair for multiplying our blessings. Therefore, let us be quick to be in the way of grace."

Thomas Chalmers

Most Christians know that we need to spend quality time with God in His Word. But, for all too many of us, the Bible is a vast and imposing book. As a result, we tend to only skim the surface of Scripture, randomly and haphazardly. Our best intentions are foiled again and again by the crowded hours of our lives, dominated by the tyranny of the urgent. Even when we, by force of sheer discipline, are able to establish regular patterns of Bible reading, retaining what we've just studied seems to be more than a little elusive.

What if there was a better way? What if there was an easier way? What if there was a way for us to not only begin to relish the riches of Scripture, incorporating those riches into our daily lives, but then to be able to help disciple others to do the same thing in their own lives? What if there was a time-tested pattern of delving into the Word of God that could help us transform our Bible knowledge—and consequently prod us on to faithful patterns of discipleship, witness, and calling?

There is. Indeed, there is a very old approach to this very old dilemma: how can we root ourselves in the deep and wondrous, life-changing truths of Scripture in a systematic and substantive fashion that is both sustainable and transferable? There is a way for us to not only grow in our own spiritual maturity, but to effectively disciple our children, our students, our friends, our coworkers, and our congregation.

Long ago, the prophet Jeremiah declared, "Thus says the Lord: 'Stand by the roads, and look, and ask for the old paths, where the good way is, and walk in it, and find rest for your souls'" (Jeremiah 6:16).

In 1811, Thomas Chalmers (1780-1847), then a young pastor in Scotland, began to glean insights from the "Old Paths" of the devotional traditions of Christendom and combined them with the "Good Way" of the Scriptural reforms of Protestantism. At first, he undertook this project to broaden his own understanding of the Gospel and to deepen his knowledge of the Word. But eventually, he would apply what he was learning to his teaching and discipling relationships. The results were immediate and profound. Over the course of the next thirty-five years, the spiritual landscape of Scotland was transformed.

According to historian Iain Murray, "When Chalmers was born in 1780 it was about the deadest time in the history of the Church of Scotland since the Reformation. When he died in 1847 it was about the alivest. The difference was almost entirely attributable to the Spirit's work through him."

Chalmers would become the undisputed leader of a vibrant Evangelical resurgence. In the coming years he would serve as pastor, professor, and publisher. He would establish schools, missions organizations, and Bible societies. He would write books on a myriad of subjects from economics and social policy to systematic theology and strategic missional extension. He would lead an unprecedented church planting movement. And, he would mentor an entire generation of theologians, pastors, educators, missionaries, writers, thinkers, scientists, politicians, and reformers.

James Cothran said, "He was of the rare order of men whose students are their children; who draw to themselves that young love which is above the love of women and by some magnetic power, bring the youths flocking to them from afar, from the very ends of the earth. He himself always young, had the Socratic love about him, the divine love for the immature, identifying them with truth and progress, which elicited their fondest regard in return. Modern universities scarcely afford a parallel; one must go back to the attractions of an Abelard or an Erasmus."

Indeed, W.M. Taylor observed, "To the end of his days he had around him a circle of loving and devoted students, all of whom were fired with enthusiasm which they had caught from his lips. He was not so much an instructor as a quickener. The other professors laid the materials in the minds of the students, but he brought and struck the match, which kindled these materials into a flame that burned with an energy kindred to his own."

His disciples proved to be a veritable galaxy of brilliant, Reformed Scots preachers, writers, and missionaries which included Robert Murray McCheyne, William Chalmers Burns, John Milne, Alexander Moody Stuart, John Urquhart, Robert Nesbit, Alexander Somerville, Rabbi John Duncan, David Ewart, Alexander Duff, William Sinclair Mackay, and the Bonar brothers John, James, Andrew, and Horatius. Emphasizing as they did a pursuit of sanctification and a passion for evangelism—both at home and abroad on the mission field— together these men came to be known variously as the "Evangelical Prodigies," the "St. Andrews Savants," the "School of the Saints," and the "Chalmers Bejants." Indeed, they would be responsible for an astonishing burst of Gospel energy, productivity, and profundity hardly ever matched before or since.

C.H. Waller claimed, "The nearest approach that I know of in the history of the Church universal to apostolic conditions of faith and living was what was to be seen in the Free Church of Scotland in its early days under the stewardship of Thomas Chalmers."

In other words, in the short span of his lifetime, Chalmers was able to launch an extraordinary movement of reformational change. And he was able to do so by discipling young men in the same "Good Way," along the "Old Paths" that he himself had trod. It was a very simple yet profound plan of directed Bible reading and strategic Bible memorization.

Though he was a prolific author of more than three dozen major works, Chalmers never published this plan for discipleship. But he did practice it for thirty-five years. And his students and family members would later describe his approach, sometimes in scrupulous detail. Testimonies of the plan's impact on their lives, families, and ministries abound. In addition, the diaries, journals, and correspondence of Chalmers offer tantalizing glimpses into the way he applied the plan to his own life and to the lives of the men, women, and children with whom he walked.

Over the past ten years, I have attempted to reproduce this simple plan—and then to implement it in my own devotional practices and in the approach I take to discipling the men, women, and children of my church and community. These notebooks are the first fruits of those labors. They are my attempt to pass on to you what Chalmers passed on to me: the "Old Paths" and the "Good Way" of Biblical discipleship.

George Grant
July, 2019

3

THE DISCIPLING VISION OF THOMAS CHALMERS

"There is no subject on which people are readier to form rash opinions than religion. The Bible is the best corrective to these. A man should sit down to it with the determination of taking his lesson just as he finds it—of founding his creed upon the sole principle of 'Thus Saieth the Lord,' and deriving his every idea and his every impression of truth from the authentic record of God's will."

Thomas Chalmers

"Let me be well instructed in the mysteries of the Kingdom, and let the Word of Christ dwell in me richly."

Thomas Chalmers

Thomas Chalmers was born in 1780 in the small fishing and trading village of Anstruther, on the south-east coast of Fife, Scotland. Faithful and confessional Scots Presbyterians, John and Elizabeth Chalmers lovingly raised Thomas and his eight brothers and five sisters in a home filled with good books, beautiful music, hard work, and practical faith.

From an early age it was evident that Chalmers was an exceedingly gifted child. At the age of three he outstripped his parents' resources and was enrolled in the local school. Then when he was just twelve he entered St. Andrew's University. Even there he proved to be a precocious learner, showing particular aptitude at mathematics.

Chalmers hoped to eventually to become a professor at the university and 1795 he entered the divinity school in order to prepare for a parallel career in the ministry. By 1799, he was ordained, but he continued to take courses at university, eventually becoming an assistant professor.

In 1803, two opportunities simultaneously presented themselves. He was offered the pastorate of the rural parish of Kilmany. He was also offered a permanent faculty post at the university teaching mathematics and science. Since Kilmany was not far from St. Andrews, he accepted both offers.

An energetic orator, he gained quick renown for his elegant sermons. And his mathematics courses were among the most popular offerings at the university. Thomas Chalmers was clearly a rising star and his fame began to spread far and wide.

There was just one problem: he was not yet converted. His was the cold and formal religion of the day: legalistic and moralistic. Despite his devout upbringing, his evident gifting, and his profound learning, he was unacquainted with Gospel of grace. As he would later testify, his was the religion of "Do this and live," and not of "Believe on the Lord Jesus Christ and thou shalt be saved."

But in 1809, he was struck by a series of unsettling bereavements. An older brother and sister were both stricken with tuberculosis. During the long period of suffering prior to their deaths, Chalmers nursed them at their bedside. The strength of their faith and their love for God utterly undid him. He was amazed by his dying brother's understanding of God's grace, and by the peace in his eyes as he was ushered into arms of Jesus.

Shortly after their deaths, Chalmers was himself stricken by illness, keeping him bed-ridden for several months. He became convinced that he too would die. In the depths of despair, he cried out to God in a manner he had never experienced before.

Chalmers eventually recovered his health—but he would never again be the same. When he returned to the little parish at Kilmany, he was a completely changed man. He had been profoundly humbled by the incongruity of his former life. He declared, "What are the objects of mathematical science? Magnitude and the proportions of magnitude. But in the foolishness of my youth, I had forgotten the two chief magnitudes: I thought not of the littleness of time and I recklessly thought not of the greatness of eternity."

Again he said, "On the system of 'Do this and live,' no peace, and even no true obedience, can ever be attained. It is 'Believe on the Lord Jesus Christ and thou shalt be saved.' When this belief enters the heart, joy and confidence enter along with it. The righteousness we try to work out for ourselves eludes our impotent grasp, and never can a soul arrive at a true and permanent rest in the pursuit of this object."

Prior to this transformation, Chalmers had been in the habit of deserting his parish during the week to teach at the university. But now he devoted himself full-time to the people of his church. He had a new appetite for the Scriptures and as a result his preaching came alive with remarkable passion and vibrancy. He took seriously the pastoral tasks of discipling and catechizing the flock entrusted to his care. Many years later, his biographer and son-in-law would note, it was at this time that Thomas "first came to know the power and preciousness of the sacred volume."

He realized he needed to study the Bible as he never had before. As he resolved in his journal, "I would learn of Thy holy oracles. I would take the sayings of the Bible simply and purely as they are and exercise myself on the trueness of these sayings."

It was at that time that he began to devise his "keystones" plan. On September 29, 1812 he wrote in his journal, "I finished this day my perusal of the New Testament by daily chapters, in which my object was to commit striking passages to memory. I mean to begin its perusal anew, in which this object shall be revised, and the object of fixing upon one sentiment of the chapter for habitual and recurring contemplation through the day shall be added to the former."

Essentially, after carefully studying a chapter of the Bible, he attempted to identify one verse from that chapter, a verse that summarized the argument of that particular portion of Scripture. These key verses, he would then commit to memory, hiding God's Word in his heart. His assumption was that if he could master just six verses, he would have internalized the flow of the argument of Ephesians, the whole arc of its theology. Likewise, in just six verses, he would have the outline of Galatians. In just sixteen verses, he would have a grasp of the theological structure of Romans. Over the course of the next thirty-five years, Chalmers would refine and revise the list of these "keystone" verses for every book in the New Testament as well as several books in the Old Testament, including the Psalms.

In the Scottish Reformed tradition, a modified version of the Medieval devotional practice of *Lectio Divina*, had long been practiced. This was originally a four-step approach to studying the Scriptures: first, *Lectio* or reading, second, *Meditatio* or thinking, third, *Oratio* or praying, and fourth *Contemplatio* or living. The method enabled believers to deeply reflect on the truth of the Scriptures and then to practically respond to it. To this approach, the Scots Reformers added an additional step: *Evangelii* or Gospel. So, a believer would take note of all the details of the whole passage, observing (*Lectio*). Then, he or she would seek to understand what those details teach, discerning (*Meditatio*). Then, the believer would pray through the passage, worshiping (*Oratio*). Next, he or she would contemplate the practical implications of the passage, applying (*Contemplatio*). And finally, the believer would ask, where are the doctrines of grace in this passage, contextualizing (*Evangelii*)?

Chalmers used this devotional exercise in his new-found love for the Scriptures. But then, once a chapter had been studied in this fashion, he capped the process by memorizing the key summary verse he had identified, thus implanting the truth of the passage in his heart.

The promises of God, the richness of the Scriptures, and the wonder of theology all came alive to him. He was transformed. And in short order, so was his little congregation as he discipled the men, women, and children of Kilmany using the same method.

Word spread. Crowds began to flock to the Fifeshire countryside to hear Chalmers preach and to witness the evangelistic and missional wonder of the revived parish. An age-old approach to Bible study, Scripture memory, and reformational discipleship was bearing extraordinary fruit.

His fame spread throughout Scotland—and soon, to the entire English-speaking world. In 1815, Chalmers was persuaded to leave his beloved Kilmany for the booming metropolis of Glasgow, then reeling from the social and cultural upheavals of the Industrial Revolution. He would serve as the pastor of the most prominent congregation in all of Scotland. There he pioneered innovative initiatives for the care of the poor and for church planting. He helped to establish missions organizations and Bible societies. He launched publishing houses and planted schools. But amidst this flurry of reforming work, he continued to disciple his family and his congregation using the Keystones method.

Years later when he would become a professor, first at his alma mater, St. Andrews, and later at the University of Edinburgh and New College Edinburgh, Chalmers continued to walk through the Scriptures with his students, always using the Keystones as the foundation for discipleship and training.

He believed that in the same way he had been stirred to extraordinary fruitfulness by this simple process of studying and memorizing God's Word, others could be, would be too. "He who truly accepts Christ as the alone foundation of his meritorious acceptance before God," he wrote, "is stimulated by the circumstances of his new condition to breathe holy purposes and to abound in holy performances. He is created anew unto good works. He is made the workmanship of God in Christ Jesus." Indeed, "The Gospel is no mere system of inert and unproductive orthodoxy." This because, "It is the office of the Holy Spirit to sanctify men," and, he asserted, "He does so largely through the tangible intermedium of the Word."

Consequently, at the time of his death in 1847, Kelton McFee would assert, "Scotland is now filled with men—and England has more than a few such—who never weary in giving utterance to their feelings when they speak of those times of happy excitement when they spent in the presence of Dr. Chalmers in Moral Philosophy or Theology in the class room while the great man himself held the mind and the soul all present in his powerful grasp. In as much as he sent forth over its surface a body of men, who if they turn not aside from the path that he sent them forward may, and with God's help will bring about the Christian regeneration of Scotland. For now every parish has a young, would-be-Chalmers."

What God's Word, by the power of God's Spirit, produced in Thomas Chalmers, it can surely produce in us. It is to that end that this Keystones notebook has been created.

As Chalmers declared, "Act up to the light that you have gotten by reading earnestly and praying importunately and striving laboriously—and to you, more will be given."

4

THE KEYSTONES METHOD:
HOW TO USE THIS BOOK

"Let me not be carried about by every wind of doctrine; and in the present reeling of opinions, let me remember that it is Thy Word alone which shall never pass away."

Thomas Chalmers

"You must not forget that though doubted, decried, and disowned, the Bible is the Word of God with power to recall a lost world from its state of exile and degeneracy and to dethrone sin from its ascendancy."

Thomas Chalmers

This volume of the Keystones covers the span of all four Gospels. You'll note that there are two pages for each chapter. On the top of the first page there is a quote from Chalmers drawn from his remarks on that chapter from his *Sabbath Scripture Readings*. On the top of the second is the Keystone verse for that chapter, in both the *King James Version* (KJV) and the *English Standard Version* (ESV). The remainder of the journaling space on both pages offers room for you to reflect and respond to the chapter, as well as the Keystone, utilizing the Reformed Scots adaptation of the *Lectio Divina*.

REFLECT

The *Reflection* section is for *Lectio*, *Meditatio*, and *Oratio*.

As you read the Gospel chapter (*Lectio*), what do you observe?
Are there repeated words, noteworthy images, strong verbs,
Old Testament allusions, unusual vocabulary, names, places,
promises, commands, or warnings? Take note of these and
write them down.

Then, think through what the chapter is teaching (*Meditatio*).
What does it mean? How should it be understood? How
should the passage be interpreted? Is it primarily indicative
(helping us to *see* something) or imperative (commanding us
to *do* something)? Reflect and journal your insights.

Finally, stop to pray through the whole passage (*Oratio*). What
is there to be thankful for here? How does this prompt us
to worship? Are there matters we need to ask God to give
us the grace to do or to be? Record your supplications and
intercessions.

RESPOND

Once you've reflected on the chapter, now it is time to respond to it. The *Respond* section is for *Contemplatio*, *Evangelii*, and *Memoria*.

Now, the truths of the chapter need to be practically applied (*Contemplatio*). Is there a command I need to obey, a grace I need to appropriate, a promise I need to cling to, a love I need to foster, a conviction I need to heed, or a kindness I need to extend? Write it down: but be tangible and specific—this is the place for practical application after all.

In all this, we need to be able to see the Gospel in the text (*Evangelii*). Where is the pattern of redemption shown, the glory of grace extended, the promise of forgiveness established, and the merit of Jesus laid upon us? Most of us are naturally inclined to works righteousness, so where in this passage is the corrective of sovereign grace? See it? Write it down.

Finally, commit the Keystone verse to memory (*Memoria*). How does this verse seem to summarize the chapter? How does the verse fit into the overall narrative arc of the book up to this point? In what ways does hiding this verse in our hearts shape us more and more in the image of Christ our Savior?

So how quickly should a believer attempt to work through the Keystones? Every person is different, but typically Chalmers had his students attempt to work through just two chapters a week—that's two memory verses, two sets of reflection exercises, and two sets of response exercises each week. Some may want to move a little more briskly. Some may want to pare down the workload to just one chapter per week. However you choose to do it, just do it!

Educational methodologies have demonstrated repeatedly that journaling and recitation are among the most powerful disciplines we can implement to grow in knowledge, understanding, and competency. So, utilizing the Keystones in our personal devotions can make a dramatic impact on our individual spiritual maturity.

But, perhaps even more significantly, when used in a discipling relationship, these disciplines can be transformational. The experience of Chalmers and his disciples offer a clear testimony of that.

The Keystones provide a clear pattern and expectation for both the disciple and the discipler. Hold one another accountable. Listen to the recitation of one another's memory verses. Discuss insights from the journal entries each of you have made. Talk through the Gospel implications of the passage. Use the journal entries as prompts for family devotions. Group Bible studies can be an opportunity to share breakthroughs and aha moments.

Chalmers implored, "May Thy grace open a way for Thy Word to our hearts, and strengthen us to act upon it. Let me not be carried about by every wind of doctrine; and in the present reeling of opinions, let me remember that it is Thy Word alone which shall never pass away."

To which we can only say, "Amen and amen!"

5

ACTS THROUGH PHILEMON

"Choose Him, then, my brethren. Choose Him as the Captain of your salvation. Let Him enter into your hearts by faith, and let Him dwell continually there. Cultivate a daily intercourse and a growing acquaintance with Him. O, you are in safe company, indeed, when your fellowship is with Him."

Thomas Chalmers

ACTS 1

Let me forget not, that not only did the disciples obey our Lord in going to Jerusalem, and waiting there, but that there they continued in prayer and supplication. His promise did not supersede their prayer, but rather supplied them with the very topic which formed the subject of their prayer, and gave them the encouragement, and the warrant- nay, laid on them the duty to supplicate for its fulfilment.- "For this shall be inquired after."

Thomas Chalmers

REFLECT

LECTIO: READ
observation & knowledge

MEDITATIO: THINK
interpretation & discernment

ORATIO: PRAY
intercession & worship

KEYSTONE

You will receive power when the Holy Spirit has come upon you, and you will be My witnesses in Jerusalem and in all Judea and Samaria, and to the end of the earth. (ESV)

But ye shall receive power, after that the Holy Ghost is come upon you: and ye shall be witnesses unto me both in Jerusalem, and in all Judaea, and in Samaria, and unto the uttermost part of the earth. (KJV)

Acts 1:8

RESPOND

CONTEMPLATIO: LIVE   *application & integration*

EVANGELII: GOSPEL   *contextualization & grace*

MEMORIA: MEMORIZE   *enscripturate & engrain*

ACTS 2

O may Christ be at my right hand, and I shall not be moved, Let my tongue speak of his righteousness, and my heart therein rejoice, Make me full of joy, O God, with the light of Thy reconciled countenance.

Thomas Chalmers

REFLECT

LECTIO: READ

observation & knowledge

MEDITATIO: THINK

interpretation & discernment

ORATIO: PRAY

intercession & worship

KEYSTONE

They devoted themselves to the apostles' teaching and the fellowship, to the breaking of bread and the prayers. (ESV)

And they continued stedfastly in the apostles' doctrine and fellowship, and in breaking of bread, and in prayers. (KJV)

Acts 2:42

RESPOND

CONTEMPLATIO: LIVE   *application & integration*

EVANGELII: GOSPEL   *contextualization & grace*

MEMORIA: MEMORIZE   *enscripturate & engrain*

ACTS 3

O God, do Thou loose my own bands- do Thou set me at liberty, that emancipated from the guilt and the power of sin, I may go forth with heaven-born alacrity in all the services of righteousness, to the praise of Thy grace: and let me ascribe nothing to any power or holiness of my own. And may I remember what the channel is through which this grace cometh- even faith in the name of Christ.

Thomas Chalmers

REFLECT

LECTIO: READ

observation & knowledge

MEDITATIO: THINK

interpretation & discernment

ORATIO: PRAY

intercession & worship

KEYSTONE

God, having raised up His servant, sent Him to you first, to bless you by turning every one of you from your wickedness. (ESV)

Unto you first God, having raised up his Son Jesus, sent him to bless you, in turning away every one of you from his iniquities. (KJV)

Acts 3:26

RESPOND

CONTEMPLATIO: LIVE   *application & integration*

EVANGELII: GOSPEL   *contextualization & grace*

MEMORIA: MEMORIZE   *enscripturate & engrain*

ACTS 4

There is nothing new under the sun. As in former days, so now, might there again be the opposition of this world's rulers to the preaching of a pure and a free Gospel. Grant us, O Lord, the same recompense which the Apostles had before us, so that howbeit despised and thwarted by men in place and in power, many might believe on the word spoken by the upright and intrepid expounders of the truth as it is in Jesus.

Thomas Chalmers

_____ REFLECT _____

LECTIO: READ   *observation & knowledge*

MEDITATIO: THINK   *interpretation & discernment*

ORATIO: PRAY   *intercession & worship*

KEYSTONE

There is salvation in no one else, for there is no other name under heaven given among men by which we must be saved. (ESV)

Neither is there salvation in any other: for there is none other name under heaven given among men, whereby we must be saved.(KJV)

Acts 4:12

RESPOND

CONTEMPLATIO: LIVE
application & integration

EVANGELII: GOSPEL
contextualization & grace

MEMORIA: MEMORIZE
enscripturate & engrain

ACTS 5

Sanctify, O God, the principle of all our doings, and let their effect be the turning of many to righteousness. Let the impellent power and motive of our proceeding be obedience to God rather than to men; yet, let not a feeling of proud resistance to man, or triumph over him, taint and vitiate this sacred influence.

Thomas Chalmers

REFLECT

LECTIO: READ

observation & knowledge

MEDITATIO: THINK

interpretation & discernment

ORATIO: PRAY

intercession & worship

KEYSTONE

We must obey God rather than men. (ESV)

We ought to obey God rather than men. (KJV)

Acts 5:29b

RESPOND

CONTEMPLATIO: LIVE

application & integration

EVANGELII: GOSPEL

contextualization & grace

MEMORIA: MEMORIZE

enscripturate & engrain

ACTS 6

Pour, O God, the Spirit of grace and supplication on our Church's office-bearers; and while Thou providest labourers in the more high and heavenly work heralding from our pulpits the salvation of the New Testament, we pray that all the other needful offices of the Church may be abundantly and completely filled. More especially do we pray for a sufficient supply of deacons, who might relieve the ministers of all the secularities which are too often accumulated upon them.

Thomas Chalmers

REFLECT

LECTIO: READ
observation & knowledge

MEDITATIO: THINK
interpretation & discernment

ORATIO: PRAY
intercession & worship

We will devote ourselves to prayer and to the ministry of the Word. (ESV)

But we will give ourselves continually to prayer, and to the ministry of the word. (KJV)

Acts 6:4

RESPOND

CONTEMPLATIO: LIVE   *application & integration*

EVANGELII: GOSPEL   *contextualization & grace*

MEMORIA: MEMORIZE   *enscripturate & engrain*

ACTS 7

The worthies of the Old Testament had much to endure from their enemies, and these chiefly their own countrymen. Such were the perversities of God's chosen people, and such their hostile and malicious treatment of the prophets and holy men of old. Let us not count it strange should our own days witness the same exhibition; but if the Lord be with us, as He was with His servants under the Hebrew dispensation, who can be against us?

Thomas Chalmers

REFLECT

LECTIO: READ

observation & knowledge

MEDITATIO: THINK

interpretation & discernment

ORATIO: PRAY

intercession & worship

KEYSTONE

You stiff-necked people, uncircumcised in heart and ears, you always resist the Holy Spirit. (ESV)

Ye stiffnecked and uncircumcised in heart and ears, ye do always resist the Holy Ghost. (KJV)

Acts 7:51a

RESPOND

CONTEMPLATIO: LIVE

application & integration

EVANGELII: GOSPEL

contextualization & grace

MEMORIA: MEMORIZE

enscripturate & engrain

ACTS 8

O that the Gospel were proclaimed in purity and with power all over the land: And O that it proved to me the harbinger both of gladness and of sanctification. May it light up joy in my heart, while, at the same time, it purges out all my uncleanness. O that I were holy in all my thoughts and ways, and had that spiritual-mindedness which is life and peace.

Thomas Chalmers

REFLECT

LECTIO: READ

observation & knowledge

MEDITATIO: THINK

interpretation & discernment

ORATIO: PRAY

intercession & worship

KEYSTONE

Peter said to him, "May your silver perish with you, because you thought you could obtain the gift of God with money!" (ESV)

But Peter said unto him, Thy money perish with thee, because thou hast thought that the gift of God may be purchased with money. (KJV)

Acts 8:20

RESPOND

CONTEMPLATIO: LIVE   *application & integration*

EVANGELII: GOSPEL   *contextualization & grace*

MEMORIA: MEMORIZE   *enscripturate & engrain*

ACTS 9

Jesus Christ, make me whole. Cure me of my spiritual diseases, and may the law of the Spirit of life in Thee make me free from the law of sin and death. Fill me with the Christian grace of liberality, and that both for the bodies and the souls of men.

Thomas Chalmers

REFLECT

LECTIO: READ
observation & knowledge

MEDITATIO: THINK
interpretation & discernment

ORATIO: PRAY
intercession & worship

KEYSTONE

So the church throughout all Judea and Galilee and Samaria had peace and was being built up. And walking in the fear of the Lord and in the comfort of the Holy Spirit, it multiplied. (ESV)

Then had the churches rest throughout all Judaea and Galilee and Samaria, and were edified; and walking in the fear of the Lord, and in the comfort of the Holy Ghost, were multiplied. (KJV)

Acts 9:31

RESPOND

CONTEMPLATIO: LIVE   *application & integration*

EVANGELII: GOSPEL   *contextualization & grace*

MEMORIA: MEMORIZE   *enscripturate & engrain*

ACTS 10

Let me be liberalized by this whole contemplation, of God cleansing that which before was common, and taking into acceptance those who in our contracted view might be regarded as outcasts and aliens. There is a certain style of evangelism which limits the Gospel economy, and would obliterate the largeness and liberality by which it is characterized.

Thomas Chalmers

REFLECT

LECTIO: READ

observation & knowledge

MEDITATIO: THINK

interpretation & discernment

ORATIO: PRAY

intercession & worship

KEYSTONE

Truly I understand that God shows no partiality. (ESV)

Of a truth I perceive that God is no respecter of persons. (KJV)

Acts 10:34b

RESPOND

CONTEMPLATIO: LIVE   *application & integration*

EVANGELII: GOSPEL   *contextualization & grace*

MEMORIA: MEMORIZE   *enscripturate & engrain*

ACTS 11

Faith gives acceptance to our prayers- for it is whatsoever we ask believingly, in the same of Christ, that we receive; and the Holy Spirit is peculiarly and pre-eminently a gift which is promised to them who ask Him- Under His blessed inspiration may we be willing to distribute and ready to communicate.

Thomas Chalmers

REFLECT

LECTIO: READ

observation & knowledge

MEDITATIO: THINK

interpretation & discernment

ORATIO: PRAY

intercession & worship

KEYSTONE

What God has made clean, do not call common. (ESV)

What God hath cleansed, that call not thou common. (KJV)

Acts 11:9b

RESPOND

CONTEMPLATIO: LIVE
application & integration

EVANGELII: GOSPEL
contextualization & grace

MEMORIA: MEMORIZE
enscripturate & engrain

ACTS 12

Vindicate Thy people's freedom; and grant that the fetters which now bind the circulation of Thy Gospel may fall away or be broken in pieces. Deliver us, O Lord, from the hand of those who would enslave the souls and consciences of men and disappoint their expectations who predict our speedy downfall, and are exulting in the prospect of their own triumphant victory over us. Let our weapons be prayer and patience; nor let either our sufferings, or our toils, tempt us away from the charity of the Gospel.

Thomas Chalmers

REFLECT

LECTIO: READ

observation & knowledge

MEDITATIO: THINK

interpretation & discernment

ORATIO: PRAY

intercession & worship

KEYSTONE

The word of God increased and multiplied. (ESV)

But the word of God grew and multiplied. (KJV)

Acts 12:24

RESPOND

CONTEMPLATIO: LIVE

application & integration

EVANGELII: GOSPEL

contextualization & grace

MEMORIA: MEMORIZE

enscripturate & engrain

ACTS 13

These glorious overtures which have come to us from Heaven are limited to none. They were to the Jew first, but also to the Gentiles. Draw me, o Lord, to the Saviour; enable me to close with the offered grace, and to continue therein; begin the good work, and carry it onward to perfection; let me not only be rooted in Christ but built up in Him, even to the measure of the stature of a perfect man in Christ Jesus my Lord.

Thomas Chalmers

REFLECT

LECTIO: READ

observation & knowledge

MEDITATIO: THINK

interpretation & discernment

ORATIO: PRAY

intercession & worship

Let it be known to you therefore, brothers, that through this Man forgiveness of sins is proclaimed to you, and by Him everyone who believes is freed from everything from which you could not be freed by the Law of Moses. ESV)

Be it known unto you therefore, men and brethren, that through this man is preached unto you the forgiveness of sins: and by him all that believe are justified from all things, from which ye could not be justified by the law of Moses. (KJV)

Acts 13:38-39

RESPOND

CONTEMPLATIO: LIVE

application & integration

EVANGELII: GOSPEL

contextualization & grace

MEMORIA: MEMORIZE

enscripturate & engrain

ACTS 14

O enable me for all the services of the new obedience of the Gospel, that I may run in the way of Thy commandments, and offer with joy and thankfulness such spiritual sacrifices as are acceptable in Thy sight.

Thomas Chalmers

REFLECT

LECTIO: READ

observation & knowledge

MEDITATIO: THINK

interpretation & discernment

ORATIO: PRAY

intercession & worship

KEYSTONE

Through many tribulations we must enter the kingdom of God. (ESV)

We must through much tribulation enter into the kingdom of God. (KJV)

Acts 14:22b

RESPOND

CONTEMPLATIO: LIVE
application & integration

EVANGELII: GOSPEL
contextualization & grace

MEMORIA: MEMORIZE
enscripturate & engrain

ACTS 15

It is indeed a doctrine very full of comfort, that we are justified by faith alone; but not, as has been well said, by a faith which is alone. It is a faith which purifies the heart, and so followed up by the fruits of holiness. We are saved by grace, but yet a grace which both teaches and enables us to deny ungodliness and worldly lusts. Let this be our great achievement, putting off the yoke of carnal ordinances.

Thomas Chalmers

REFLECT

LECTIO: READ

observation & knowledge

MEDITATIO: THINK

interpretation & discernment

ORATIO: PRAY

intercession & worship

KEYSTONE

For it has seemed good to the Holy Spirit and to us to lay on you no greater burden than these requirements. (ESV)

For it seemed good to the Holy Ghost, and to us, to lay upon you no greater burden than these necessary things. (KJV)

Acts 15:28

RESPOND

CONTEMPLATIO: LIVE
application & integration

EVANGELII: GOSPEL
contextualization & grace

MEMORIA: MEMORIZE
enscripturate & engrain

ACTS 16

Let us, within the limits of principle and duty, be all things to all men; and O that such was our wisdom, and such our charity, as that under the instrumentality of both, and by God's blessing, the true Churches of our land were more and more established, and that they increased in number daily.

Thomas Chalmers

REFLECT

LECTIO: READ

observation & knowledge

MEDITATIO: THINK

interpretation & discernment

ORATIO: PRAY

intercession & worship

The jailer cried out, "Sirs, what must I do to be saved?" And they said, "Believe in the Lord Jesus, and you will be saved, you and your household." (ESV)

Sirs, what must I do to be saved? And they said, Believe on the Lord Jesus Christ, and thou shalt be saved, and thy house. (KJV)

Acts 16:30b-31

RESPOND

CONTEMPLATIO: LIVE   *application & integration*

EVANGELII: GOSPEL   *contextualization & grace*

MEMORIA: MEMORIZE   *enscripturate & engrain*

Let me compare scriptural things with scriptural, which is in fact comparing spiritual things with spiritual. Thence I shall gather that there was not only a 'need be' for the sufferings of Christ, in that it was so foretold in Scripture- and all its sayings must be fulfilled- but a 'need be' for an atonement in the deep-laid necessities of Heaven's jurisprudence, and the divine character.

Thomas Chalmers

REFLECT

LECTIO: READ

observation & knowledge

MEDITATIO: THINK

interpretation & discernment

ORATIO: PRAY

intercession & worship

KEYSTONE

In Him we live and move and have our being. (ESV)

For in him we live, and move, and have our being. (KJV)

Acts 17:28a

RESPOND

CONTEMPLATIO: LIVE
application & integration

EVANGELII: GOSPEL
contextualization & grace

MEMORIA: MEMORIZE
enscripturate & engrain

ACTS 18

Let me be a follower of Paul in his unwearied activity for the furtherance of the Gospel, and let me cheerfully resign any right of my own to a temporal remuneration for my services. O help mine unbelief, and give me, Lord, the unspeakable comfort of all who are in my house believing along with me. And let me be intrepid of utterance when declaring the free Gospel of the grace of God. Let me not be afraid, but speak, and hold not my peace.

Thomas Chalmers

_____ REFLECT _____

LECTIO: READ   *observation & knowledge*

MEDITATIO: THINK   *interpretation & discernment*

ORATIO: PRAY   *intercession & worship*

KEYSTONE

Do not be afraid, but go on speaking and do not be silent. (ESV)

Be not afraid, but speak, and hold not thy peace. (KJV)

Acts 18:9b

RESPOND

CONTEMPLATIO: LIVE   *application & integration*

EVANGELII: GOSPEL   *contextualization & grace*

MEMORIA: MEMORIZE   *enscripturate & engrain*

ACTS 19

O perform within me the miracles of Thine all-subduing grace, that I may become a new creature, and walk in newness of life and heart before Thee. And may Thy word, O Lord, be paramount with me to all other wisdom. Let all the ingenuities of human speculation, and all its curiosities, give way before the overbearing yet rightful authority of- "Thus saith the Lord."

Thomas Chalmers

REFLECT

LECTIO: READ

observation & knowledge

MEDITATIO: THINK

interpretation & discernment

ORATIO: PRAY

intercession & worship

KEYSTONE

The Word of the Lord continued to increase and prevail mightily. (ESV)

So mightily grew the word of God and prevailed. (KJV)

Acts 19:20

RESPOND

CONTEMPLATIO: LIVE   *application & integration*

EVANGELII: GOSPEL   *contextualization & grace*

MEMORIA: MEMORIZE   *enscripturate & engrain*

ACTS 20

O for more zeal and industry in my Master's work. Awaken me, O Lord, to a right conscientiousness in the great object of spreading abroad the knowledge of salvation. O that I attained to the earnestness of the apostle, who labored in birth till Christ was formed in his converts, and was moved even to tears in his longing desire after their salvation. Give me, O Lord, to teach aright both repentance and faith.

Thomas Chalmers

REFLECT

LECTIO: READ

observation & knowledge

MEDITATIO: THINK

interpretation & discernment

ORATIO: PRAY

intercession & worship

It is more blessed to give than to receive. (ESV)

It is more blessed to give than to receive. (KJV)

Acts 20:35b

RESPOND

CONTEMPLATIO: LIVE   *application & integration*

EVANGELII: GOSPEL   *contextualization & grace*

MEMORIA: MEMORIZE   *enscripturate & engrain*

ACTS 21

Let me be a follower of Paul, both in that he committed his journeying and the wellbeing of those from whom he separated to Thee by prayer, and in that he was ready to do all and to suffer all for the name of the Lord Jesus. Let me also follow him in his liberal accommodation to the prejudices of others- distinguishing aright between liberality and liberalism, between accommodations of Christian wisdom and charity on the one hand, and all sinful compliances on the other.

Thomas Chalmers

REFLECT

LECTIO: READ
observation & knowledge

MEDITATIO: THINK
interpretation & discernment

ORATIO: PRAY
intercession & worship

KEYSTONE

Let the will of the Lord be done. (ESV)

The will of the Lord be done. (KJV)

Acts 21:14b

RESPOND

CONTEMPLATIO: LIVE

application & integration

EVANGELII: GOSPEL

contextualization & grace

MEMORIA: MEMORIZE

enscripturate & engrain

ACTS 22

Let me not be content either with a zeal without knowledge, or a knowledge without zeal. Let me not only refrain from all coldness or hostility to the servants of Christ, but honour and do service to them as such- seeing that I should thus do honour and service to Christ.

Thomas Chalmers

REFLECT

LECTIO: READ

observation & knowledge

MEDITATIO: THINK

interpretation & discernment

ORATIO: PRAY

intercession & worship

KEYSTONE

Now why do you wait? Rise and be baptized and wash away your sins, calling on His name. (ESV)

And now why tarriest thou? arise, and be baptized, and wash away thy sins, calling on the name of the Lord. (KJV)

Acts 22:16

RESPOND

CONTEMPLATIO: LIVE   *application & integration*

EVANGELII: GOSPEL   *contextualization & grace*

MEMORIA: MEMORIZE   *enscripturate & engrain*

ACTS 23

My God, what I know not teach Thou me; and more especially do I pray both for guidance and grace. Teach me, O Lord, to beware of the leaven of the Sadducees, and still more to beware of being a Pharisee in form while a Sadducee in practice. O that I felt at all times the cheering effect of my Saviour's Gospel.

Thomas Chalmers

REFLECT

LECTIO: READ

observation & knowledge

MEDITATIO: THINK

interpretation & discernment

ORATIO: PRAY

intercession & worship

The following night the Lord stood by him and said, "Take courage, for as you have testified to the facts about me in Jerusalem, so you must testify also in Rome." (ESV)

And the night following the Lord stood by him, and said, Be of good cheer, Paul: for as thou hast testified of me in Jerusalem, so must thou bear witness also at Rome. (KJV)

Acts 23:11

RESPOND

CONTEMPLATIO: LIVE
application & integration

EVANGELII: GOSPEL
contextualization & grace

MEMORIA: MEMORIZE
enscripturate & engrain

ACTS 24

It is truly instructive to read of the topics which formed Paul's address to Felix. He spake concerning the faith in Christ, and when so doing, reasoned of righteousness, temperance, and judgement- that is, on the commandments of the law and final reckonings of the law, making use of the law as a schoolmaster for bringing his hearer unto Christ.

Thomas Chalmers

REFLECT

LECTIO: READ

observation & knowledge

MEDITATIO: THINK

interpretation & discernment

ORATIO: PRAY

intercession & worship

KEYSTONE

This I confess to you, that according to the Way, which they call a sect, I worship the God of our fathers, believing everything laid down by the Law and written in the Prophets, having a hope in God, which these men themselves accept. (ESV)

But this I confess unto thee, that after the way which they call heresy, so worship I the God of my fathers, believing all things which are written in the law and in the prophets: And have hope toward God, which they themselves also allow. (KJV)

Acts 24:14-15a

RESPOND

CONTEMPLATIO: LIVE   *application & integration*

EVANGELII: GOSPEL   *contextualization & grace*

MEMORIA: MEMORIZE   *enscripturate & engrain*

ACTS 25

How completely apart from each other the two policies are of the Church and of the world; and yet how so adapted to each other as to subserve the government of Him who worketh all in all.

Thomas Chalmers

REFLECT

LECTIO: READ

observation & knowledge

MEDITATIO: THINK

interpretation & discernment

ORATIO: PRAY

intercession & worship

KEYSTONE

Paul argued in his defense, "Neither against the law of the Jews, nor against the temple, nor against Caesar have I committed any offense." (ESV)

While he answered for himself, Neither against the law of the Jews, neither against the temple, nor yet against Caesar, have I offended anything at all. (KJV)

Acts 25:8

RESPOND

CONTEMPLATIO: LIVE   *application & integration*

EVANGELII: GOSPEL   *contextualization & grace*

MEMORIA: MEMORIZE   *enscripturate & engrain*

ACTS 26

Grant, O Lord, such manifestations of Thyself as might lead me to see in bright perspective the things of an unseen world; open Thou mine eyes, and turn me from darkness unto light, and from the power of Satan unto God. Ever blessed be Thy name that Thou hast made known so clearly the instrument of our satisfaction- even the faith that is in Christ.

Thomas Chalmers

REFLECT

LECTIO: READ

observation & knowledge

MEDITATIO: THINK

interpretation & discernment

ORATIO: PRAY

intercession & worship

KEYSTONE

Agrippa said to Paul, "In so short a time would you persuade me to be a Christian?" (ESV)

Then Agrippa said unto Paul, Almost thou persuadest me to be a Christian. (KJV)

Acts 26:28

RESPOND

CONTEMPLATIO: LIVE   *application & integration*

EVANGELII: GOSPEL   *contextualization & grace*

MEMORIA: MEMORIZE   *enscripturate & engrain*

ACTS 27

O let me labour to make any calling and election sure. Let me be enabled to superadd the assurance of experience to the assurance of faith; and meanwhile let me be of good cheer when I bethink myself of that proffered mercy in Gospel which is held forth to all, and which all have a warrant to lay hold of.

Thomas Chalmers

REFLECT

LECTIO: READ

observation & knowledge

MEDITATIO: THINK

interpretation & discernment

ORATIO: PRAY

intercession & worship

KEYSTONE

Take heart, men. (ESV)

Wherefore, sirs, be of good cheer. (KJV)

Acts 27:25a

RESPOND

CONTEMPLATIO: LIVE   *application & integration*

EVANGELII: GOSPEL   *contextualization & grace*

MEMORIA: MEMORIZE   *enscripturate & engrain*

ACTS 28

Let us take courage in Him who will not leave us defenseless in the work of spreading abroad His truth, even throughout the families of a hostile world.

Thomas Chalmers

REFLECT

LECTIO: READ

observation & knowledge

MEDITATIO: THINK

interpretation & discernment

ORATIO: PRAY

intercession & worship

KEYSTONE

Therefore let it be known to you that this salvation of God has been sent to the Gentiles; they will listen. (ESV)

Be it known therefore unto you, that the salvation of God is sent unto the Gentiles, and that they will hear it. (KJV)

Acts 28:28

RESPOND

CONTEMPLATIO: LIVE   *application & integration*

EVANGELII: GOSPEL   *contextualization & grace*

MEMORIA: MEMORIZE   *enscripturate & engrain*

ROMANS 1

And let me not be ashamed of the Gospel of Christ. Let me experience it as Thy power unto salvation; and may the righteousness of faith which is therein revealed be received by me so submissively and believingly as to become my righteousness unto spiritual life here and everlasting life hereafter.

Thomas Chalmers

REFLECT

LECTIO: READ

observation & knowledge

MEDITATIO: THINK

interpretation & discernment

ORATIO: PRAY

intercession & worship

KEYSTONE

I am not ashamed of the Gospel, for it is the power of God for salvation to everyone who believes, to the Jew first and also to the Greek. For in it the righteousness of God is revealed from faith for faith, as it is written, "The righteous shall live by faith." (ESV)

For I am not ashamed of the gospel of Christ: for it is the power of God unto salvation to everyone that believeth; to the Jew first, and also to the Greek. For therein is the righteousness of God revealed from faith to faith: as it is written, the just shall live by faith. (KJV)

Romans 1:16-17

RESPOND

CONTEMPLATIO: LIVE
application & integration

EVANGELII: GOSPEL
contextualization & grace

MEMORIA: MEMORIZE
enscripturate & engrain

O let me delay no longer to avail myself of this my season of grace and opportunity, while God still forbears the infliction of deserved wrath, and still waiteth to be gracious. Let this goodness lead me to repentance; for how shall I escape if I neglect these overtures of a salvation so great and precious? Convince me of sin. Shut me up unto the Saviour. May I close with Him as my surety and High Priest, yet bear a constant and practical regard to Him as my Master and my Judge.

Thomas Chalmers

REFLECT

LECTIO: READ
observation & knowledge

MEDITATIO: THINK
interpretation & discernment

ORATIO: PRAY
intercession & worship

Do you despise the riches of His kindness, restraint, and patience not recognizing that God's kindness is intended to lead you to repentance? (ESV)

Or despisest thou the riches of His goodness and forbearance and longsuffering; not knowing that the goodness of God leadeth thee to repentance? (KJV)

Romans 2:4

RESPOND

CONTEMPLATIO: LIVE
application & integration

EVANGELII: GOSPEL
contextualization & grace

MEMORIA: MEMORIZE
enscripturate & engrain

Surely my mouth is stopped; and I can allege nothing against the sentence of my entire and most righteous condemnation. This is what the Law brings me to when sitting as a Judge; but when giving forth its lessons as a schoolmaster, the same law brings me to Christ. He hath done what the law could not do, in that it was weak through the flesh. He hath brought in a righteousness that is without the law- that it, a righteousness not coming out of our obedience to the law, but a righteousness brought in by Christ and made ours by faith. O my God, let me draw water abundantly out of this well of salvation. O how cheerfully do I renounce all merit of my own, that Christ may be my sufficiency and all my dependence.

Thomas Chalmers

REFLECT

LECTIO: READ
observation & knowledge

MEDITATIO: THINK
interpretation & discernment

ORATIO: PRAY
intercession & worship

KEYSTONE

All have sinned and fall short of the glory of God, and are justified by His grace as a gift, through the redemption that is in Christ Jesus. (ESV)

For all have sinned, and come short of the glory of God; Being justified freely by His grace through the redemption that is in Christ Jesus. (KJV)

Romans 3:23-24

RESPOND

CONTEMPLATIO: LIVE
application & integration

EVANGELII: GOSPEL
contextualization & grace

MEMORIA: MEMORIZE
enscripturate & engrain

ROMANS 4

Give me, O Lord, the blessedness of him whose sins are forgiven, whose iniquities are covered, and, still more, to whom the Lord imputeth- without works of his own, a positive and perfect righteousness. O the blessedness of that new condition which is announced in the Gospel- even that my safety and God's glory are at one- so that all is mine if I believe in Him that raised Jesus from the dead, who was given up as an offering for my offences; and now that He is an Advocate and Intercessor at the Father's right hand, there pleads for my interest and claim in that everlasting righteousness which Himself brought in.

Thomas Chalmers

REFLECT

LECTIO: READ

observation & knowledge

MEDITATIO: THINK

interpretation & discernment

ORATIO: PRAY

intercession & worship

KEYSTONE

What does the Scripture say? "Abraham believed God, and it was counted to him as righteousness." (ESV)

For what saith the scripture? Abraham believed God, and it was counted unto him for righteousness. (KJV)

Romans 4:3

RESPOND

CONTEMPLATIO: LIVE   *application & integration*

EVANGELII: GOSPEL   *contextualization & grace*

MEMORIA: MEMORIZE   *enscripturate & engrain*

ROMANS 5

He who died for us when enemies will not abandon is now that we are friends, or earnestly seeking after His friendship. But why seek as if in uncertainty any longer? Let us henceforth rejoice in Christ, as in a treasure that hath been found- and not only so, but also joy in God through Him by whom we have received the Atonement.

Thomas Chalmers

REFLECT

LECTIO: READ
observation & knowledge

MEDITATIO: THINK
interpretation & discernment

ORATIO: PRAY
intercession & worship

KEYSTONE

God shows His love for us in that while we were still sinners, Christ died for us. (ESV)

But God commendeth His love toward us, in that, while we were yet sinners, Christ died for us. (KJV)

Romans 5:8

RESPOND

CONTEMPLATIO: LIVE   *application & integration*

EVANGELII: GOSPEL   *contextualization & grace*

MEMORIA: MEMORIZE   *enscripturate & engrain*

ROMANS 6

Deliver me, O God, from the reigning power of sin. May the law of the Spirit of life in Christ Jesus make me free from the law of sin and death.

Thomas Chalmers

REFLECT

LECTIO: READ

observation & knowledge

MEDITATIO: THINK

interpretation & discernment

ORATIO: PRAY

intercession & worship

KEYSTONE

The wages of sin is death, but the free gift of God is eternal life in Christ Jesus our Lord. (ESV)

For the wages of sin is death; but the gift of God is eternal life through Jesus Christ our Lord. (KJV)

Romans 6:23

RESPOND

CONTEMPLATIO: LIVE   *application & integration*

EVANGELII: GOSPEL   *contextualization & grace*

MEMORIA: MEMORIZE   *enscripturate & engrain*

113

Deliver me, O Lord, from vile concupiscence- still more vile, that it should be excited and take occasion by Thy good and pure and holy Law. How exceeding sinful, then, is sin. Give me, O Lord, to mourn not with a sorrow transient and unproductive, but with a real practical and Godly sorrow- a working sorrow, even that which worketh repentance unto salvation.

Thomas Chalmers

REFLECT

LECTIO: READ
observation & knowledge

MEDITATIO: THINK
interpretation & discernment

ORATIO: PRAY
intercession & worship

Wretched man that I am! Who will deliver me from this body of death? Thanks be to God through Jesus Christ our Lord! (ESV)

O wretched man that I am! Who shall deliver me from the body of this death? I thank God through Jesus Christ our Lord. (KJV)

Romans 7:24-25a

RESPOND

CONTEMPLATIO: LIVE   *application & integration*

EVANGELII: GOSPEL   *contextualization & grace*

MEMORIA: MEMORIZE   *enscripturate & engrain*

ROMANS 8

O may His love to me not only ensure His protection amid all the ills and distresses of life, but may it so constrain my love to Him, that no calamities, no terrors, no temptations, shall ever cause me to swerve from the fidelity and gratitude which I owe to that blessed Saviour who died for me, and who rose again- who died for my offences, and rose again for my justification. Give me to be strong, yea, and more than conqueror over these three great enemies to the human souls- the devil, and the world, and the flesh.

Thomas Chalmers

REFLECT

LECTIO: READ
observation & knowledge

MEDITATIO: THINK
interpretation & discernment

ORATIO: PRAY
intercession & worship

KEYSTONE

There is therefore now no condemnation for those who are in Christ Jesus. (ESV)

There is therefore now no condemnation to them which are in Christ Jesus. (KJV)

Romans 8:1

RESPOND

CONTEMPLATIO: LIVE

application & integration

EVANGELII: GOSPEL

contextualization & grace

MEMORIA: MEMORIZE

enscripturate & engrain

ROMANS 9

Oh that I had the same affection for the souls of kindred and neighbours which actuated the holy apostle. Give me, O Lord, more and more of what may well be termed the benevolence of faith. Let me learn a prostrate subjection of all my faulties and feelings to God's truth and God's sovereignty.

Thomas Chalmers

REFLECT

LECTIO: READ

observation & knowledge

MEDITATIO: THINK

interpretation & discernment

ORATIO: PRAY

intercession & worship

KEYSTONE

The Lord said to Moses, "I will have mercy on whom I have mercy, and I will have compassion on whom I have compassion." So then it depends not on human will or exertion, but on God, who has mercy. (ESV)

For He saith to Moses, I will have mercy on whom I will have mercy, and I will have compassion on whom I will have compassion. So then it is not of him that willeth, nor of him that runneth, but of God that sheweth mercy. (KJV)

Romans 9:15-16

RESPOND

CONTEMPLATIO: LIVE
application & integration

EVANGELII: GOSPEL
contextualization & grace

MEMORIA: MEMORIZE
enscripturate & engrain

ROMANS 10

Faith ever cometh by hearing or by reading the word of God; and I would therefore give earnest heed unto this word, till the day dawn, and the day-star arise in my heart. My the beautiful feet of them who preach the Gospel of peace pervade the whole length and breadth of the land, and so as thoroughly to fill it, from one end to the other, with the tabernacles of the righteous.

Thomas Chalmers

REFLECT

LECTIO: READ
observation & knowledge

MEDITATIO: THINK
interpretation & discernment

ORATIO: PRAY
intercession & worship

KEYSTONE

Faith comes from hearing, and hearing through the Word of Christ. (ESV)

So then faith cometh by hearing, and hearing by the word of God. (KJV)

Romans 10:17

RESPOND

CONTEMPLATIO: LIVE

application & integration

EVANGELII: GOSPEL

contextualization & grace

MEMORIA: MEMORIZE

enscripturate & engrain

We rejoice in the clear and definite line of separation, which is drawn between grace and works. Salvation is of grace only, and not of works at all; but still of grace unto works. Let me never be distrustful of my own strength and my own sufficiency; and may I ever be looking upward for support and aid to that place whence the aliment of spiritual life alone comes.

Thomas Chalmers

REFLECT

LECTIO: READ

observation & knowledge

MEDITATIO: THINK

interpretation & discernment

ORATIO: PRAY

intercession & worship

KEYSTONE

Oh, the depth of the riches and wisdom and knowledge of God! How unsearchable are His judgments and how inscrutable His ways! (ESV)

O the depth of the riches both of the wisdom and knowledge of God! How unsearchable are His judgments, and His ways past finding out! (KJV)

Romans 11:33

RESPOND

CONTEMPLATIO: LIVE

application & integration

EVANGELII: GOSPEL

contextualization & grace

MEMORIA: MEMORIZE

enscripturate & engrain

ROMANS 12

First and foremost, O God, give me to keep this vile body under subjection, and present it to Thee as a living sacrifice acceptable to God through Jesus Christ my Lord: and O renovate and transform me- that henceforth I may walk before Thee a new creature; then shall I do Thy will, not of constraint by spontaneously.

Thomas Chalmers

REFLECT

LECTIO: READ
observation & knowledge

MEDITATIO: THINK
interpretation & discernment

ORATIO: PRAY
intercession & worship

I appeal to you therefore, brothers, by the mercies of God, to present your bodies as a living sacrifice, holy and acceptable to God, which is your spiritual worship. Do not be conformed to this world but be transformed by the renewing of your minds so that you may be able to prove what the will of God is, what is good and acceptable and perfect. (ESV)

I beseech you therefore, brethren, by the mercies of God, that ye present your bodies a living sacrifice, holy, acceptable unto God, which is your reasonable service. And be not conformed to this world: but be ye transformed by the renewing of your mind, that ye may prove what is that good, and acceptable, and perfect, will of God. (KJV)

Romans 12:1-2

RESPOND

CONTEMPLATIO: LIVE   *application & integration*

EVANGELII: GOSPEL   *contextualization & grace*

MEMORIA: MEMORIZE   *enscripturate & engrain*

Surely it is high time for me to awake. My time in this world of darkness is far spent, and another world is at hand. Let me come forth on the broad daylight of a Christian practice harmonizing at all points with a Christian profession.

Thomas Chalmers

REFLECT

LECTIO: READ   *observation & knowledge*

MEDITATIO: THINK   *interpretation & discernment*

ORATIO: PRAY   *intercession & worship*

KEYSTONE

Owe no one anything, except to love each other, for the one who loves another has fulfilled the Law. (ESV)

Owe no man any thing, but to love one another: for he that loveth another hath fulfilled the law. (KJV)

Romans 13:8

RESPOND

CONTEMPLATIO: LIVE
application & integration

EVANGELII: GOSPEL
contextualization & grace

MEMORIA: MEMORIZE
enscripturate & engrain

Teach me, O Lord, to discriminate aright, essential, nor lay undue stress on what is insignificant. We must content earnestly for the faith, and all the weightier matters, whether of doctrinal or practical Christianity; but why endanger unity and the peace of the Church for the veriest bagatelles.

Thomas Chalmers

REFLECT

LECTIO: READ

observation & knowledge

MEDITATIO: THINK

interpretation & discernment

ORATIO: PRAY

intercession & worship

KEYSTONE

Let us pursue what makes for peace and for mutual up-building. (ESV)

Let us therefore follow after the things which make for peace, and things wherewith one may edify another. (KJV)

Romans 14:19

RESPOND

CONTEMPLATIO: LIVE

application & integration

EVANGELII: GOSPEL

contextualization & grace

MEMORIA: MEMORIZE

enscripturate & engrain

ROMANS 15

Let us make a sacrifice of our own will to the great interests both of truth and charity. Let us imitate Christ in His self-denial, and always please others rather than ourselves when it is for their profit. Let us be likeminded with Him, and so likeminded one toward another.

Thomas Chalmers

REFLECT

LECTIO: READ

observation & knowledge

MEDITATIO: THINK

interpretation & discernment

ORATIO: PRAY

intercession & worship

KEYSTONE

May the God of hope fill you with all joy and peace in believing, so that by the power of the Holy Spirit you may abound in hope. (ESV)

Now the God of hope fill you with all joy and peace in believing, that ye may abound in hope, through the power of the Holy Ghost. (KJV)

Romans 15:13

RESPOND

CONTEMPLATIO: LIVE   *application & integration*

EVANGELII: GOSPEL   *contextualization & grace*

MEMORIA: MEMORIZE   *enscripturate & engrain*

ROMANS 16

May the God of Peace bruise Satan under my feet, and may the graces of the Lord Jesus Christ be with me; and thus may I realize in my own person both the peace of the Gospel and the holiness of the Gospel.

Thomas Chalmers

REFLECT

LECTIO: READ

observation & knowledge

MEDITATIO: THINK

interpretation & discernment

ORATIO: PRAY

intercession & worship

KEYSTONE

The God of peace will soon crush Satan under your feet. The grace of our Lord Jesus Christ be with you. (ESV)

And the God of peace shall bruise Satan under your feet shortly. The grace of our Lord Jesus Christ be with you. Amen. (KJV)

Romans 16:20

RESPOND

CONTEMPLATIO: LIVE   *application & integration*

EVANGELII: GOSPEL   *contextualization & grace*

MEMORIA: MEMORIZE   *enscripturate & engrain*

I CORINTHIANS 1

My God, save our Church from divisions. If there be differences of understanding, let there be no divisions of heart amongst our rules and office-bearers. Let us shun partisanship; and instead of ranging ourselves under men, let us, with all simplicity and Godly sincerity, seek after the mind of God and the good of His Church, and abide thereby. O may the preaching of this Cross be the power of God to me and mine.

Thomas Chalmers

REFLECT

LECTIO: READ

observation & knowledge

MEDITATIO: THINK

interpretation & discernment

ORATIO: PRAY

intercession & worship

KEYSTONE

God is faithful, by whom you were called into the fellowship of his Son, Jesus Christ our Lord. (ESV)

God is faithful, by whom ye were called unto the fellowship of his Son Jesus Christ our Lord. (KJV)

I Corinthians 1:9

RESPOND

CONTEMPLATIO: LIVE   *application & integration*

EVANGELII: GOSPEL   *contextualization & grace*

MEMORIA: MEMORIZE   *enscripturate & engrain*

I CORINTHIANS 2

O let mine be the glorious determination of the apostle- to know nothing save Jesus Christ and Him crucified; let Him be all my all in all; and in the work of making Him known to others, may I have a deep sense of my own insufficiency for the work. But O give me to experience that when I am weak then I am strong; let me be led to the Rock that is higher than I; drawing from Scripture for my words; but more than this, drawing by prayer for the grace from heaven, which alone can make there effectual.

Thomas Chalmers

REFLECT

LECTIO: READ

observation & knowledge

MEDITATIO: THINK

interpretation & discernment

ORATIO: PRAY

intercession & worship

KEYSTONE

The natural person does not accept the things of the Spirit of God, for they are folly to him, and he is not able to understand them because they are spiritually discerned. (ESV)

But the natural man receiveth not the things of the Spirit of God: for they are foolishness unto him: neither can he know them, because they are spiritually discerned. (KJV)

I Corinthians 2:14

RESPOND

CONTEMPLATIO: LIVE   *application & integration*

EVANGELII: GOSPEL   *contextualization & grace*

MEMORIA: MEMORIZE   *enscripturate & engrain*

I CORINTHIANS 3

O Lord, may we be of Thy husbandry and of Thy building; and, whether for ourselves of others, while we labour with all diligence both in planting and watering, both I casting of the seed of God's word upon the soul and in praying for living water from heaven to fertilize it, let us ever over look above our own efforts and our own prayers to Him out of whose fullness it it that all fertility comes; and let us build on no other foundation than that which God Himself hath laid in Zion.

Thomas Chalmers

REFLECT

LECTIO: READ

observation & knowledge

MEDITATIO: THINK

interpretation & discernment

ORATIO: PRAY

intercession & worship

For the wisdom of this world is folly with God. (ESV)

For the wisdom of this world is foolishness with God. For it is written, He taketh the wise in their own craftiness. (KJV)

I Corinthians 3:19

RESPOND

CONTEMPLATIO: LIVE   *application & integration*

EVANGELII: GOSPEL   *contextualization & grace*

MEMORIA: MEMORIZE   *enscripturate & engrain*

O may God save me from glorifying in myself. Thou art the great fountain-head of all I have, and of all I am. Perfect within me the grace of humility; may I ever be clothed therewith. Give me the spirit of love, and of power, and of a sound mind; give me to feel practically and in its governing influence the truth as it is in Jesus, that I may be sanctified by that truth.

Thomas Chalmers

REFLECT

LECTIO: READ

observation & knowledge

MEDITATIO: THINK

interpretation & discernment

ORATIO: PRAY

intercession & worship

KEYSTONE

For the kingdom of God does not consist in talk but in power. (ESV)

For the kingdom of God is not in word, but in power. (KJV)

I Corinthians 4:20

RESPOND

CONTEMPLATIO: LIVE   *application & integration*

EVANGELII: GOSPEL   *contextualization & grace*

MEMORIA: MEMORIZE   *enscripturate & engrain*

141

My God, restore to me the joys of thy salvation, and make me glad in the light of Thy reconciled countenance; and save me-save me from that willful sinning after which there remaineth no more sacrifice for sins, but a certain fearful looking for of judgement.

Thomas Chalmers

REFLECT

LECTIO: READ

observation & knowledge

MEDITATIO: THINK

interpretation & discernment

ORATIO: PRAY

intercession & worship

KEYSTONE

Do you not know that a little leaven leavens the whole lump? (ESV)

Know ye not that a little leaven leaveneth the whole lump? (KJV)

I Corinthians 5:6

RESPOND

CONTEMPLATIO: LIVE   *application & integration*

EVANGELII: GOSPEL   *contextualization & grace*

MEMORIA: MEMORIZE   *enscripturate & engrain*

I CORINTHIANS 6

Let me never lose sight of the truth that I am not my won, but the property and at the absolute disposal of Him who bought me. His are both my body and my spirit, and in these let me glorify Him whose they are, being alike their Maker and their Preserver.

Thomas Chalmers

REFLECT

LECTIO: READ
observation & knowledge

MEDITATIO: THINK
interpretation & discernment

ORATIO: PRAY
intercession & worship

KEYSTONE

You are not your own, for you were bought with a price. So glorify God in your body. (ESV)

What? know ye not that your body is the temple of the Holy Ghost which is in you, which ye have of God, and ye are not your own? For ye are bought with a price: therefore glorify God in your body, and in your spirit, which are God's. (KJV)

I Corinthians 6:19-20

RESPOND

CONTEMPLATIO: LIVE
application & integration

EVANGELII: GOSPEL
contextualization & grace

MEMORIA: MEMORIZE
enscripturate & engrain

I CORINTHIANS 7

Let me sit loose to the enjoyments of this world- and on the consideration too that the time is short, and the world soon passeth away. Let this both moderate my attachment to the pleasures of life, and make its disappointment and crosses fall light upon me. Whatever I do let it be in the Lord.

Thomas Chalmers

REFLECT

LECTIO: READ

observation & knowledge

MEDITATIO: THINK

interpretation & discernment

ORATIO: PRAY

intercession & worship

KEYSTONE

Only let each person lead the life that the Lord has assigned to him, and to which God has called him. (ESV)

But as God hath distributed to every man, as the Lord hath called every one, so let him walk. And so ordain I in all churches. (KJV)

I Corinthians 7:17

RESPOND

CONTEMPLATIO: LIVE   *application & integration*

EVANGELII: GOSPEL   *contextualization & grace*

MEMORIA: MEMORIZE   *enscripturate & engrain*

I CORINTHIANS 8

Keep me, O Lord, within the limits of a sound and sober Christian philosophy. Deliver me from all imagination of my own sufficiency, and more particularly of my knowledge.

Thomas Chalmers

REFLECT

LECTIO: READ

observation & knowledge

MEDITATIO: THINK

interpretation & discernment

ORATIO: PRAY

intercession & worship

KEYSTONE

If anyone loves God, he is known by God. (ESV)

But if any man love God, the same is known of him. (KJV)

I Corinthians 8:3

CONTEMPLATIO: LIVE   *application & integration*

EVANGELII: GOSPEL   *contextualization & grace*

MEMORIA: MEMORIZE   *enscripturate & engrain*

I CORINTHIANS 9

Let me make no secret of the undoubted doctrine, that they which preach the Gospel shall live of the Gospel. Heavenly Father, along with our aspirations after public usefulness, may we ever be careful of our own personal Christianity, lest when we preach to others we ourselves should be castaways.

Thomas Chalmers

---------------- REFLECT ----------------

LECTIO: READ   *observation & knowledge*

MEDITATIO: THINK   *interpretation & discernment*

ORATIO: PRAY   *intercession & worship*

KEYSTONE

I discipline my body and keep it under control, lest after preaching to others I myself should be disqualified. (ESV)

But I keep under my body, and bring it into subjection: lest that by any means, when I have preached to others, I myself should be a castaway. (KJV)

I Corinthians 9:27

RESPOND

CONTEMPLATIO: LIVE
application & integration

EVANGELII: GOSPEL
contextualization & grace

MEMORIA: MEMORIZE
enscripturate & engrain

I CORINTHIANS 10

O my God, let me henceforth be intent on the fulfilment of Thy will, which is my sanctification. Give me more certainly and distinctly to know my calling, that I may press toward the mark for the prize thereof. Let me not be seduced from this high walk by the temptations of any sort; and, O my God, either strengthen me for the encounter, or provide me a way of escape from them, as Thou seest to be best.

Thomas Chalmers

REFLECT

LECTIO: READ

observation & knowledge

MEDITATIO: THINK

interpretation & discernment

ORATIO: PRAY

intercession & worship

KEYSTONE

No temptation has overtaken you that is not common to man. God is faithful, and He will not let you be tempted beyond your ability, but with the temptation He will also provide the way of escape, that you may be able to endure it. (ESV)

There hath no temptation taken you but such as is common to man: but God is faithful, who will not suffer you to be tempted above that ye are able; but will with the temptation also make a way to escape, that ye may be able to bear it. (KJV)

I Corinthians 10:13

RESPOND

CONTEMPLATIO: LIVE
application & integration

EVANGELII: GOSPEL
contextualization & grace

MEMORIA: MEMORIZE
enscripturate & engrain

I CORINTHIANS 11

The stimulus of a human example enforce the duty of imitating a Divine example. We are called upon to be followers of Paul, even as he was of Christ- a legitimate argument therefore, and which both demonstrates the use of holding ourselves foth as patterns to our fellow-men, and the responsibility under which we lie, for the sake of others, to maintain the walk and the conversation which become the gospel of Jesus Christ. Let my light then so shine, that others seeing my good works may be led to copy them, to the glory of my Father in Heaven.

Thomas Chalmers

---------------------------------- REFLECT ----------------------------------

LECTIO: READ
observation & knowledge

MEDITATIO: THINK
interpretation & discernment

ORATIO: PRAY
intercession & worship

KEYSTONE

For as often as you eat this bread and drink the cup, you proclaim the Lord's death until He comes. (ESV)

For as often as ye eat this bread, and drink this cup, ye do shew the Lord's death till he come. (KJV)

I Corinthians 11:26

RESPOND

CONTEMPLATIO: LIVE   *application & integration*

EVANGELII: GOSPEL   *contextualization & grace*

MEMORIA: MEMORIZE   *enscripturate & engrain*

155

I CORINTHIANS 12

Gifts are desirable and to be coveted earnestly, but graces are of far higher worth than gifts, and of far higher importance to the wellbeing both of the Church and of society.

Thomas Chalmers

REFLECT

LECTIO: READ

observation & knowledge

MEDITATIO: THINK

interpretation & discernment

ORATIO: PRAY

intercession & worship

KEYSTONE

To each is given the manifestation of the Spirit for the common good. (ESV)

But the manifestation of the Spirit is given to every man to profit withal. (KJV)

I Corinthians 12:7

RESPOND

CONTEMPLATIO: LIVE

application & integration

EVANGELII: GOSPEL

contextualization & grace

MEMORIA: MEMORIZE

enscripturate & engrain

I CORINTHIANS 13

Let me lay up treasure for Heaven, and be sustained by a view of the mighty enlargements of knowledge and power which await me there, where all the dimness, and misunderstandings, and consequent mutual reviling's, which take place in our controversies below, shall all be dissipated in the pure and ethereal light of those higher regions where knowledge shall be perfected, and where faith and hope shall be left behind as but forever remain in the paradise of God.

Thomas Chalmers

REFLECT

LECTIO: READ

observation & knowledge

MEDITATIO: THINK

interpretation & discernment

ORATIO: PRAY

intercession & worship

KEYSTONE

Love bears all things, believes all things, hopes all things, endures all things. (ESV)

Beareth all things, believeth all things, hopeth all things, endureth all things. (KJV)

I Corinthians 13:7

RESPOND

CONTEMPLATIO: LIVE   *application & integration*

EVANGELII: GOSPEL   *contextualization & grace*

MEMORIA: MEMORIZE   *enscripturate & engrain*

Never, O Lord, let my trumpet sound uncertainly- never let me aspire after such a language as might prove an unknown tongue to the common people. Pardon, O God, my every wrong and vain effort at the wisdom of words. Let me preach not as a man of gifts—unintelligible to many- but as a man of grace, commending myself to the consciences of all.

Thomas Chalmers

REFLECT

LECTIO: READ

observation & knowledge

MEDITATIO: THINK

interpretation & discernment

ORATIO: PRAY

intercession & worship

KEYSTONE

All things should be done decently and in order. (ESV)

Let all things be done decently and in order. (KJV)

I Corinthians 14:40

CONTEMPLATIO: LIVE   *application & integration*

EVANGELII: GOSPEL   *contextualization & grace*

MEMORIA: MEMORIZE   *enscripturate & engrain*

I CORINTHIANS 15

Faith without memory is vain- that is, the things believed are of no use to us unless they are called to remembrance and dwelt upon by the mind. Let me recur with the greatest fondness and frequency yea, ever and anon, to the precious doctrine of Scripture, that Christ died for my sins- and thus may a clear conscience, and a confident apprehension of God as my reconciled Father, be at all times upheld within me; and let me also be ever thinking of him as my risen Saviour. Let me keep a firm hold by faith of His resurrection, and be conformed thereto by a spiritual resurrection in own soul from sin unto godliness.

Thomas Chalmers

REFLECT

LECTIO: READ

observation & knowledge

MEDITATIO: THINK

interpretation & discernment

ORATIO: PRAY

intercession & worship

KEYSTONE

Therefore, my beloved brothers, be steadfast, immovable, always abounding in the work of the Lord, knowing that in the Lord your labor is not in vain. (ESV)

Therefore, my beloved brethren, be ye stedfast, unmoveable, always abounding in the work of the Lord, forasmuch as ye know that your labour is not in vain in the Lord. (KJV)

I Corinthians 15:58

RESPOND

CONTEMPLATIO: LIVE

application & integration

EVANGELII: GOSPEL

contextualization & grace

MEMORIA: MEMORIZE

enscripturate & engrain

I CORINTHIANS 16

Truth fortitude are qualified with the winning and attractive grace of charity. Let us stand fast and contend earnestly for the faith once delivered to the saints; let us be manly and strenuous in the vindication thereof; and yet let all our things be done with charity.

Thomas Chalmers

REFLECT

LECTIO: READ

observation & knowledge

MEDITATIO: THINK

interpretation & discernment

ORATIO: PRAY

intercession & worship

KEYSTONE

Be watchful, stand firm in the faith, act like men, be strong. Let all that you do be done in love. (ESV)

Watch ye, stand fast in the faith, quit you like men, be strong. Let all your things be done with charity. (KJV)

I Corinthians 16:13-14

RESPOND

CONTEMPLATIO: LIVE   *application & integration*

EVANGELII: GOSPEL   *contextualization & grace*

MEMORIA: MEMORIZE   *enscripturate & engrain*

II CORINTHIANS 1

The God of all comfort leaves us at the times to a period of tribulation and trial; and thus our lives may alternate between joy and sorrow. Let our trust not be in ourselves but in Him- that like as He raised Christ from the dead, so He, the Father of Christ, may raise us from a state of heaviness and suffering to a state of enlargement and triumph. In this faith, and by this faith, O God, may I ever stand.

Thomas Chalmers

REFLECT

LECTIO: READ

observation & knowledge

MEDITATIO: THINK

interpretation & discernment

ORATIO: PRAY

intercession & worship

KEYSTONE

Blessed be the God and Father of our Lord Jesus Christ, the Father of mercies and God of all comfort, who comforts us in all our affliction, so that we may be able to comfort those who are in any affliction, with the comfort with which we ourselves are comforted by God. (ESV)

Blessed be God, even the Father of our Lord Jesus Christ, the Father of mercies, and the God of all comfort; Who comforteth us in all our tribulation, that we may be able to comfort them which are in any trouble, by the comfort wherewith we ourselves are comforted of God. (KJV)

II Corinthians 1:3-4

RESPOND

CONTEMPLATIO: LIVE   *application & integration*

EVANGELII: GOSPEL   *contextualization & grace*

MEMORIA: MEMORIZE   *enscripturate & engrain*

II CORINTHIANS 2

Be at peace with me, O God, and restore peace to my conscience. Let me never distrust the efficacy of my Saviour's blood; but O satisfy me with present evidence of my being His. Give me this token of my having indeed trusted in Christ- my being sealed with the Holy Spirit of promise, that Spirit which not only lusteth against the flesh, but prevails over it.

Thomas Chalmers

REFLECT

LECTIO: READ

observation & knowledge

MEDITATIO: THINK

interpretation & discernment

ORATIO: PRAY

intercession & worship

KEYSTONE

For we are the aroma of Christ to God among those who are being saved and among those who are perishing, to one a fragrance from death to death, to the other a fragrance from life to life. Who is sufficient for these things? (ESV)

For we are unto God a sweet savour of Christ, in them that are saved, and in them that perish: To the one we are the savour of death unto death; and to the other the savour of life unto life. And who is sufficient for these things? (KJV)

II Corinthians 2:15-16

RESPOND

CONTEMPLATIO: LIVE   *application & integration*

EVANGELII: GOSPEL   *contextualization & grace*

MEMORIA: MEMORIZE   *enscripturate & engrain*

II CORINTHIANS 3

Take, O Lord, the heart of stone out of me, and make it a heart of flesh, soft, tender, and susceptible of a deep and enduring impression from Thy holy word. Make Thy grace sufficient through Thy Spirit pressing home upon my mind those lessons of that knowledge of God and Jesus Christ, which is life everlasting.

Thomas Chalmers

REFLECT

LECTIO: READ

observation & knowledge

MEDITATIO: THINK

interpretation & discernment

ORATIO: PRAY

intercession & worship

KEYSTONE

Our sufficiency is from God. (ESV)

But our sufficiency is of God. (KJV)

II Corinthians 3:5

RESPOND

CONTEMPLATIO: LIVE

application & integration

EVANGELII: GOSPEL

contextualization & grace

MEMORIA: MEMORIZE

enscripturate & engrain

Give me a full assurance of understanding to the acknowledgement of the mystery of God and of the Father and of Christ. (Col ii.2) Give me the light of the knowledge of Thy glory in the face of Jesus Christ, and in his great work of redemption. Lift the veil from my mind that it may be in darkness no longer, but that in Thy light I clearly see light.

Thomas Chalmers

_____ REFLECT _____

LECTIO: READ
observation & knowledge

MEDITATIO: THINK
interpretation & discernment

ORATIO: PRAY
intercession & worship

KEYSTONE

We have this treasure in jars of clay, to show that the surpassing power belongs to God and not to us. (ESV)

But we have this treasure in earthen vessels, that the excellency of the power may be of God, and not of us. (KJV)

II Corinthians 4:7

RESPOND

CONTEMPLATIO: LIVE   *application & integration*

EVANGELII: GOSPEL   *contextualization & grace*

MEMORIA: MEMORIZE   *enscripturate & engrain*

II CORINTHIANS 5

What a basis for the evangelical obedience of new creatures in Jesus Christ! What a mighty change is implied in our becoming Christians!- with new aims, new habits, new affections, new objects of pursuit; and yet what a free opening to this great enlargement- this vast revolution in the character and state of man. All is of God, who bestows the power to enter upon and preserve in this altogether new life; and who most welcomeley, and with perfect good-will, invites us to the commencement of this new era in our moral and spiritual history.

Thomas Chalmers

REFLECT

LECTIO: READ

observation & knowledge

MEDITATIO: THINK

interpretation & discernment

ORATIO: PRAY

intercession & worship

KEYSTONE

We walk by faith, not by sight. (ESV)

For we walk by faith, not by sight. (KJV)

II Corinthians 5:7

RESPOND

CONTEMPLATIO: LIVE

application & integration

EVANGELII: GOSPEL

contextualization & grace

MEMORIA: MEMORIZE

enscripturate & engrain

II CORINTHIANS 6

If we, in very deed receive Christ, we shall receive along with Him power to be and to do as the children of God. Let us come out then from a world lying in wickedness; let us keep at a distance from all that is evil; let us touch not and tamper not with temptation.

Thomas Chalmers

REFLECT

LECTIO: READ

observation & knowledge

MEDITATIO: THINK

interpretation & discernment

ORATIO: PRAY

intercession & worship

Behold, now is the favorable time; behold, now is the day of salvation. (ESV)

For he saith, I have heard thee in a time accepted, and in the day of salvation have I succoured thee: behold, now is the accepted time; behold, now is the day of salvation. (KJV)

II Corinthians 6:2

RESPOND

CONTEMPLATIO: LIVE

application & integration

EVANGELII: GOSPEL

contextualization & grace

MEMORIA: MEMORIZE

enscripturate & engrain

Though we have the promises we are not therefore exempted from the precepts; nay, the one is an argument, and the very consideration for urging on our obedience to the other. May I hence forward rest with unfaltering reliance on the offered privileges of the Gospel, and because so resting and so relying, may I now count it and proceed upon it as my unceasing business, to perfect my holiness in the fear of God. Enable me, Almighty Father, thoroughly to cleanse myself, not from the flesh only, but from what good old Boston calls, speculative impurity. Do thou purge even my sorrow for sin of all its selfishness.

Thomas Chalmers

REFLECT

LECTIO: READ

observation & knowledge

MEDITATIO: THINK

interpretation & discernment

ORATIO: PRAY

intercession & worship

Behold, now is the accepted time; behold, now is the day of salvation. Godly grief produces a repentance that leads to salvation without regret, whereas worldly grief produces death. (ESV)

For godly sorrow worketh repentance to salvation not to be repented of: but the sorrow of the world worketh death. (KJV)

II Corinthians 7:10

RESPOND

CONTEMPLATIO: LIVE   *application & integration*

EVANGELII: GOSPEL   *contextualization & grace*

MEMORIA: MEMORIZE   *enscripturate & engrain*

II CORINTHIANS 8

Bestow on me in larger measure and proportion that grace which Thou didst so plentifully bestow on the churches of Macedonia. Let it spread abroad more and more. It is still but a day of small things. O do Thou brighten it onward even unto the latter day glory.

Thomas Chalmers

REFLECT

LECTIO: READ

observation & knowledge

MEDITATIO: THINK

interpretation & discernment

ORATIO: PRAY

intercession & worship

You know the grace of our Lord Jesus Christ, that though He was rich, yet for your sake He became poor, so that you by His poverty might become rich. (ESV)

For ye know the grace of our Lord Jesus Christ, that, though He was rich, yet for your sakes He became poor, that ye through His poverty might be rich. (KJV)

II Corinthians 8:9

RESPOND

CONTEMPLATIO: LIVE

application & integration

EVANGELII: GOSPEL

contextualization & grace

MEMORIA: MEMORIZE

enscripturate & engrain

181

II CORINTHIANS 9

Let the duty giving be better understood, and more felt and acted on in this our day. In this department, too, of Christian obedience, let the duty, even as all duty should, be our delight. And God is not unrighteous to forget our work and labour of love. Let us sow bountifully and we shall reap bountifully; yet let it not be in mercenary hope of a reward that we let forth our liberality on the objects of Christian benevolence.

Thomas Chalmers

REFLECT

LECTIO: READ

observation & knowledge

MEDITATIO: THINK

interpretation & discernment

ORATIO: PRAY

intercession & worship

God loves a cheerful giver. (ESV)

For God loveth a cheerful giver. (KJV)

II Corinthians 9:7

RESPOND

CONTEMPLATIO: LIVE   *application & integration*

EVANGELII: GOSPEL   *contextualization & grace*

MEMORIA: MEMORIZE   *enscripturate & engrain*

II CORINTHIANS 10

Let me hope that I am now disabused of the false confidence which might be suggested by the comparison of myself with my fellow-men. Even on the ground of this comparison there is much to humble me, and when I look at the patience, and the courteousness, and the hospitality, even of unconverted men, there is great reason why I should feel abashed, and put the question to my conscience. Elevate me, O Lord, from the terrestrial to the celestial contemplation- from the moralities of an earthly to those of a heavenly and Divine citizenship. Stablish us in Christ, that rooted and built up in Him we may attain to the fullness of the stature of perfect men in Christ Jesus our Lord.

Thomas Chalmers

REFLECT

LECTIO: READ
observation & knowledge

MEDITATIO: THINK
interpretation & discernment

ORATIO: PRAY
intercession & worship

KEYSTONE

The weapons of our warfare are not of the flesh but have divine power to destroy strongholds. We destroy arguments and every lofty opinion raised against the knowledge of God, and take every thought captive to obey Christ. (ESV)

For the weapons of our warfare are not carnal, but mighty through God to the pulling down of strong holds; Casting down imaginations, and every high thing that exalteth itself against the knowledge of God, and bringing into captivity every thought to the obedience of Christ. (KJV)

II Corinthians 10:4-5

RESPOND

CONTEMPLATIO: LIVE   *application & integration*

EVANGELII: GOSPEL   *contextualization & grace*

MEMORIA: MEMORIZE   *enscripturate & engrain*

II CORINTHIANS 11

Give to me and mine, O Lord, the simple trust in Him which brings down the Spirit as the earnest of our inheritance hereafter, and which also works in us here a simply and an entire devotedness to the will and glory of the great Emanuel. Let no plausibility seduce us from the direct and obvious simplicity of the truth as it in Jesus. Save me alike from the avarice and from the ostentation of its opposite.

Thomas Chalmers

REFLECT

LECTIO: READ

observation & knowledge

MEDITATIO: THINK

interpretation & discernment

ORATIO: PRAY

intercession & worship

KEYSTONE

Satan disguises himself as an angel of light. (ESV)

For Satan himself is transformed into an angel of light. (KJV)

II Corinthians 11:14

RESPOND

CONTEMPLATIO: LIVE   *application & integration*

EVANGELII: GOSPEL   *contextualization & grace*

MEMORIA: MEMORIZE   *enscripturate & engrain*

II CORINTHIANS 12

Let believing and constant supplication be my refuge, so as I may experience that when I am weak then am strong. Give me, O Lord, to realize this mystery, this great secret of practical godliness. Make Thy grace, O God, sufficient for me, perfect Thy strength in my weakness.

Thomas Chalmers

REFLECT

LECTIO: READ

observation & knowledge

MEDITATIO: THINK

interpretation & discernment

ORATIO: PRAY

intercession & worship

KEYSTONE

The Lord said, "My grace is sufficient for you, for My power is made perfect in weakness." Therefore I will boast all the more gladly of my weaknesses, so that the power of Christ may rest upon me. (ESV)

And he said unto me, My grace is sufficient for thee: for my strength is made perfect in weakness. Most gladly therefore will I rather glory in my infirmities, that the power of Christ may rest upon me. (KJV)

II Corinthians 12:9

RESPOND

CONTEMPLATIO: LIVE
application & integration

EVANGELII: GOSPEL
contextualization & grace

MEMORIA: MEMORIZE
enscripturate & engrain

II CORINTHIANS 13

Let no vile admixture of the corrupt and the carnal be present so as to vitiate or unhallow love; and O may I have the full manifestation and experience in my soul of the grace of the Lord Jesus, and the love of God, and the communion of the Holy Ghost.

Thomas Chalmers

REFLECT

LECTIO: READ
observation & knowledge

MEDITATIO: THINK
interpretation & discernment

ORATIO: PRAY
intercession & worship

KEYSTONE

Examine yourselves, to see whether you are in the faith. Test yourselves. Or do you not realize this about yourselves, that Jesus Christ is in you? Unless indeed, you fail to meet the test! (ESV)

Examine yourselves, whether ye be in the faith; prove your own selves. Know ye not your own selves, how that Jesus Christ is in you, except ye be reprobates? (KJV)

II Corinthians 13:5

RESPOND

CONTEMPLATIO: LIVE

application & integration

EVANGELII: GOSPEL

contextualization & grace

MEMORIA: MEMORIZE

enscripturate & engrain

GALATIANS 1

Let us contend earnestly for the faith once delivered to the saints; and more especially let us never falter or decline by ever so little from the precious doctrine, that by grace we are saved.

Thomas Chalmers

REFLECT

LECTIO: READ

observation & knowledge

MEDITATIO: THINK

interpretation & discernment

ORATIO: PRAY

intercession & worship

He gave Himself for our sins to deliver us from the present evil age, according to the will of our God and Father, to whom be the glory forever and ever. Amen. (ESV)

Who gave himself for our sins, that He might deliver us from this present evil world, according to the will of God and our Father: To whom be glory for ever and ever. Amen. (KJV)

Galatians 1:4-5

RESPOND

CONTEMPLATIO: LIVE   *application & integration*

EVANGELII: GOSPEL   *contextualization & grace*

MEMORIA: MEMORIZE   *enscripturate & engrain*

GALATIANS 2

Crucified with Christ, nevertheless alive, with him dead for sin, so that the law has no further claim upon us; and dead to sin, so that I no longer live in opposition to the law, but in conformity therewith, and find that in the keeping of it prescribed duties there is a very great reward, and this because Christ liveth in me, because grace and not sin hath now the dominion over me. Work, O God, this faith in me with power.

Thomas Chalmers

REFLECT

LECTIO: READ

observation & knowledge

MEDITATIO: THINK

interpretation & discernment

ORATIO: PRAY

intercession & worship

KEYSTONE

I have been crucified with Christ. It is no longer I who live, but Christ who lives in me. And the life I now live in the flesh I live by faith in the Son of God, who loved me and gave himself for me. (ESV)

I am crucified with Christ: nevertheless I live; yet not I, but Christ liveth in me: and the life which I now live in the flesh I live by the faith of the Son of God, who loved me, and gave himself for me. (KJV)

Galatians 2:20

RESPOND

CONTEMPLATIO: LIVE
application & integration

EVANGELII: GOSPEL
contextualization & grace

MEMORIA: MEMORIZE
enscripturate & engrain

GALATIANS 3

Let me look unto Jesus, and with unfaltering confidence in the efficacy of His death as a propitiation for me sins. O let me never work for a righteousness by the law, but with simply reliance on the atonement and righteousness of Christ may I be enabled, by the shedding forth upon me of the Holy Ghost, to a abound in all those fruits of the new obedience against which there is no law. May the uses of the law be still realized upon us; may it shut us up unto faith; may it act as a schoolmaster for bringing us to Christ; may it convince us of sin, and so constrain us to the Saviour.

Thomas Chalmers

REFLECT

LECTIO: READ
observation & knowledge

MEDITATIO: THINK
interpretation & discernment

ORATIO: PRAY
intercession & worship

In Christ Jesus you are all sons of God, through faith. (ESV)

For ye are all the children of God by faith in Christ Jesus. (KJV)

Galatians 3: 26

CONTEMPLATIO: LIVE   *application & integration*

EVANGELII: GOSPEL   *contextualization & grace*

MEMORIA: MEMORIZE   *enscripturate & engrain*

GALATIANS 4

O for the experimental realization of my being indeed under the glorious law of liberty. My God, emancipate my slavish heart from the dominion of weak and beggarly elements, yet so as that I shall not use my liberty as an occasion for the flesh. May I love Thy Sabbaths, and then in keeping them I shall but observe the law of liberty. Let me abound more and more in all the fruits of a willing and so a free and fearless obedience.

Thomas Chalmers

REFLECT

LECTIO: READ
observation & knowledge

MEDITATIO: THINK
interpretation & discernment

ORATIO: PRAY
intercession & worship

Now you, brothers, like Isaac, are children of promise. (ESV)

Now we, brethren, as Isaac was, are the children of promise. (KJV)

Galatians 4:28

RESPOND

CONTEMPLATIO: LIVE
application & integration

EVANGELII: GOSPEL
contextualization & grace

MEMORIA: MEMORIZE
enscripturate & engrain

GALATIANS 5

O God, do Thou renew our will, do Thou make us willing in the day of Thy power for that which is right; and then, if liberty consist in doing what we will, we shall indeed manifest the most glorious of all liberty by our abounding in all righteousness and goodness and truth.

Thomas Chalmers

REFLECT

LECTIO: READ

observation & knowledge

MEDITATIO: THINK

interpretation & discernment

ORATIO: PRAY

intercession & worship

KEYSTONE

The fruit of the Spirit is love, joy, peace, patience, kindness, goodness, faithfulness, gentleness, self-control; against such things there is no law. (ESV)

But the fruit of the Spirit is love, joy, peace, longsuffering, gentleness, goodness, faith, meekness, temperance: against such there is no law. (KJV)

Galatians 5:22-23

RESPOND

CONTEMPLATIO: LIVE   *application & integration*

EVANGELII: GOSPEL   *contextualization & grace*

MEMORIA: MEMORIZE   *enscripturate & engrain*

GALATIANS 6

Let me have a firm and deep foundation in that which God Himself hath laid in Zion- not in the vain observances of a ritual now passed away, but in that glorious atonement, by the faith in which the world loses its charms, and we die unto the world- so as to effect an entire personal transformation that makes us new creatures in Jesus Christ our Lord.

Thomas Chalmers

REFLECT

LECTIO: READ

observation & knowledge

MEDITATIO: THINK

interpretation & discernment

ORATIO: PRAY

intercession & worship

KEYSTONE

Bear one another's burdens, and so fulfill the law of Christ. (ESV)

Bear ye one another's burdens, and so fulfil the law of Christ. (KJV)

Galatians 6:2

RESPOND

CONTEMPLATIO: LIVE   *application & integration*

EVANGELII: GOSPEL   *contextualization & grace*

MEMORIA: MEMORIZE   *enscripturate & engrain*

EPHESIANS 1

His predestination is the source ad fountain-head of all, and His glory, even the glory of His grace, is the end of all; yet this larger connexion between the prime and the ultimate does not exclude from his view the nearer connexions. Our union with Christ, our acceptance in him, our redemption through His blood, even the forgiveness of sins, and all through the medium of our faith in the Saviour after that we had heard of Him, after which again cometh the sealing of the Spirit who is the earnest of our inheritance.

Thomas Chalmers

REFLECT

LECTIO: READ

observation & knowledge

MEDITATIO: THINK

interpretation & discernment

ORATIO: PRAY

intercession & worship

Blessed be the God and Father of our Lord Jesus Christ, who has blessed us in Christ with every spiritual blessing in the heavenly places. (ESV)

Blessed be the God and Father of our Lord Jesus Christ, who hath blessed us with all spiritual blessings in heavenly places in Christ. (KJV)

Ephesians 1:3

RESPOND

CONTEMPLATIO: LIVE
application & integration

EVANGELII: GOSPEL
contextualization & grace

MEMORIA: MEMORIZE
enscripturate & engrain

EPHESIANS 2

If I am indeed one of Thy chosen ones, it is not because I have worked, but have been worked upon, and so made Thy workmanship, and created by Thee in Christ Jesus, the alone foundation on which I would build, both or a right and a righteous.

Thomas Chalmers

--------------------------- REFLECT ---------------------------

LECTIO: READ

observation & knowledge

MEDITATIO: THINK

interpretation & discernment

ORATIO: PRAY

intercession & worship

KEYSTONE

By grace you have been saved through faith. And this is not your own doing; it is the gift of God, not a result of works, so that no one may boast. For we are His workmanship, created in Christ Jesus for good works, which God prepared beforehand, that we should walk in them. (ESV)

For by grace are ye saved through faith; and that not of yourselves: it is the gift of God: Not of works, lest any man should boast. For we are his workmanship, created in Christ Jesus unto good works, which God hath before ordained that we should walk in them. (KJV)

Ephesians 2:8-10

RESPOND

CONTEMPLATIO: LIVE
application & integration

EVANGELII: GOSPEL
contextualization & grace

MEMORIA: MEMORIZE
enscripturate & engrain

EPHESIANS 3

O God, let me have the experience of this great and purchased blessing- let me have the subjective experience of it, even the experience of being strengthened in the inner man with might by the Spirit, and of having Christ to dwell in my heart by faith.

Thomas Chalmers

REFLECT

LECTIO: READ
observation & knowledge

MEDITATIO: THINK
interpretation & discernment

ORATIO: PRAY
intercession & worship

KEYSTONE

Now to Him who is able to do far more abundantly than all that we ask or think, according to the power at work within us, to Him be glory in the church and in Christ Jesus throughout all generations, forever and ever. Amen. (ESV)

Now unto Him that is able to do exceeding abundantly above all that we ask or think, according to the power that worketh in us, unto Him be glory in the church by Christ Jesus throughout all ages, world without end. Amen. (KJV)

Ephesians 3:20-21

RESPOND

CONTEMPLATIO: LIVE   *application & integration*

EVANGELII: GOSPEL   *contextualization & grace*

MEMORIA: MEMORIZE   *enscripturate & engrain*

EPHESIANS 4

O my God, do Thou uphold my goings that I may walk in the truth, and walk worthy of Thee unto all well-pleasing. And I most earnestly pray for the progress and the perfecting of Christian unity- for which purpose grant that I may ever study to repress all those controversies which relate not to contend earnestly.

Thomas Chalmers

REFLECT

LECTIO: READ

observation & knowledge

MEDITATIO: THINK

interpretation & discernment

ORATIO: PRAY

intercession & worship

Speaking the truth in love, we are to grow up in every way into Him who is the head, into Christ. (ESV)

But speaking the truth in love, may grow up into Him in all things, which is the head, even Christ. (KJV)

Ephesians 4:15

RESPOND

CONTEMPLATIO: LIVE   *application & integration*

EVANGELII: GOSPEL   *contextualization & grace*

MEMORIA: MEMORIZE   *enscripturate & engrain*

EPHESIANS 5

The days are evil- for many things occur to break in on the great work of preparation for heaven. Let me therefore gather up all the fragments of time I have, and clear out as much more as I can for the one thing needful, for the growth of grace and the perfecting of holiness.

Thomas Chalmers

REFLECT

LECTIO: READ

observation & knowledge

MEDITATIO: THINK

interpretation & discernment

ORATIO: PRAY

intercession & worship

KEYSTONE

Therefore be imitators of God, as beloved children. And walk in love, as Christ loved us and gave Himself up for us, a fragrant offering and sacrifice to God. (ESV)

Be ye therefore followers of God, as dear children; And walk in love, as Christ also hath loved us, and hath given Himself for us an offering and a sacrifice to God for a sweetsmelling savour. (KJV)

Ephesians 5:1-2

RESPOND

CONTEMPLATIO: LIVE
application & integration

EVANGELII: GOSPEL
contextualization & grace

MEMORIA: MEMORIZE
enscripturate & engrain

EPHESIANS 6

Teach me, O God, the deportment I should observe in regard to my children. Let me refrain from the wrath which provoketh wrath, and which may not only irritate but also discourage them. Let mine be a calm and steady and practical regard for their souls; and let this be the manifest principle of all my dealings with them. Let me put on the requisite armour of defense and resistance, fighting him who is a spiritual for with spiritual weapons.

Thomas Chalmers

REFLECT

LECTIO: READ

observation & knowledge

MEDITATIO: THINK

interpretation & discernment

ORATIO: PRAY

intercession & worship

Be strong in the Lord and in the strength of His might. Put on the whole armor of God, that you may be able to stand against the schemes of the devil. (ESV)

Be strong in the Lord, and in the power of His might. Put on the whole armour of God, that ye may be able to stand against the wiles of the devil. (KJV)

Ephesians 6:10-11

RESPOND

CONTEMPLATIO: LIVE   *application & integration*

EVANGELII: GOSPEL   *contextualization & grace*

MEMORIA: MEMORIZE   *enscripturate & engrain*

PHILIPPIANS 1

Begin the good work of grace in my heart, and carry it onward to a full performance. Shed abroad in my heart the love of God; and let mine be an intelligent affection for the things that are above.

Thomas Chalmers

REFLECT

LECTIO: READ

observation & knowledge

MEDITATIO: THINK

interpretation & discernment

ORATIO: PRAY

intercession & worship

KEYSTONE

It is my prayer that your love may abound more and more, with knowledge and all discernment, so that you may approve what is excellent, and so be pure and blameless for the day of Christ, filled with the fruit of righteousness that comes through Jesus Christ, to the glory and praise of God. (ESV)

And this I pray, that your love may abound yet more and more in knowledge and in all judgment; That ye may approve things that are excellent; that ye may be sincere and without offence till the day of Christ; Being filled with the fruits of righteousness, which are by Jesus Christ, unto the glory and praise of God. (KJV)

Philippians 1:9-11

RESPOND

CONTEMPLATIO: LIVE   *application & integration*

EVANGELII: GOSPEL   *contextualization & grace*

MEMORIA: MEMORIZE   *enscripturate & engrain*

PHILIPPIANS 2

God works in us to set us a-working. Teach me, O Lord, to do what is right, but with a perfect freedom from that wrath which worketh not the righteousness of God, and abstinence from all grudging seeing that the Judge is at the door.

Thomas Chalmers

REFLECT

LECTIO: READ

observation & knowledge

MEDITATIO: THINK

interpretation & discernment

ORATIO: PRAY

intercession & worship

KEYSTONE

It is God who works in you, both to will and to work for His good pleasure. (ESV)

For it is God which worketh in you both to will and to do of His good pleasure. (KJV)

Philippians 2:13

RESPOND

CONTEMPLATIO: LIVE   *application & integration*

EVANGELII: GOSPEL   *contextualization & grace*

MEMORIA: MEMORIZE   *enscripturate & engrain*

PHILIPPIANS 3

Conform me, O God, to His death; and give me, O Lord, not to shrink from suffering for His sake: Above all, may I experience the power of His resurrection within me, by myself being raised to newness of life here, and so as to have part in the resurrection of blessedness from the dead hereafter.

Thomas Chalmers

REFLECT

LECTIO: READ

observation & knowledge

MEDITATIO: THINK

interpretation & discernment

ORATIO: PRAY

intercession & worship

I press on toward the goal for the prize of the upward call of God in Christ Jesus. (ESV)

I press toward the mark for the prize of the high calling of God in Christ Jesus.(KJV)

Philippians 3:14

RESPOND

CONTEMPLATIO: LIVE   *application & integration*

EVANGELII: GOSPEL   *contextualization & grace*

MEMORIA: MEMORIZE   *enscripturate & engrain*

PHILIPPIANS 4

In everything, and more especially in things of spiritual and everlasting concern, let us make our believing requests unto God, and mix thanksgiving therewith, because of the mercies and hopes and experiences of the Gospel.

Thomas Chalmers

REFLECT

LECTIO: READ

observation & knowledge

MEDITATIO: THINK

interpretation & discernment

ORATIO: PRAY

intercession & worship

KEYSTONE

Finally, brothers, whatever is true, whatever is honorable, whatever is just, whatever is pure, whatever is lovely, whatever is commendable, if there is any excellence, if there is anything worthy of praise, think about these things. What you have learned and received and heard and seen in me—practice these things, and the God of peace will be with you. (ESV)

Finally, brethren, whatsoever things are true, whatsoever things are honest, whatsoever things are just, whatsoever things are pure, whatsoever things are lovely, whatsoever things are of good report; if there be any virtue, and if there be any praise, think on these things. Those things, which ye have both learned, and received, and heard, and seen in me, do: and the God of peace shall be with you. (KJV)

Philippians 4:8-9

RESPOND

CONTEMPLATIO: LIVE   *application & integration*

EVANGELII: GOSPEL   *contextualization & grace*

MEMORIA: MEMORIZE   *enscripturate & engrain*

COLOSSIANS 1

To stablish and strengthen my faith still more, let me dwell on the greatness of Him who is the object of it- who created and sustained, and was before all things, the Lord of the universe of nature, as well as Lord of the Church: and well did He earn this latter pre-eminence, when He rose from the dead, after that by His blood He had made peace between God and man, and reconciled our race of aliens to the Lawgiver whom they had offended.

Thomas Chalmers

REFLECT

LECTIO: READ

observation & knowledge

MEDITATIO: THINK

interpretation & discernment

ORATIO: PRAY

intercession & worship

KEYSTONE

In Him all the fullness of God was pleased to dwell, and through Him to reconcile to Himself all things, whether on earth or in heaven, making peace by the blood of His cross. (ESV)

For it pleased the Father that in him should all fulness dwell; And, having made peace through the blood of His cross, by him to reconcile all things unto himself; by Him, I say, whether they be things in earth, or things in heaven. (KJV)

Colossians 1:19-20

RESPOND

CONTEMPLATIO: LIVE   *application & integration*

EVANGELII: GOSPEL   *contextualization & grace*

MEMORIA: MEMORIZE   *enscripturate & engrain*

COLOSSIANS 2

He hath loosed my bonds: let me be His servant, walking on His prescribed path, and offering the sacrifices of thanksgiving. Save me alike from the drudgeries and the hypocrisies of a vain formalism. Let mine be a spontaneous and enlightened service, emanating from that well of living water which springeth up in the heart of regenerated man, and efflorescing into all the graces and virtues of the Christian character.

Thomas Chalmers

REFLECT

LECTIO: READ

observation & knowledge

MEDITATIO: THINK

interpretation & discernment

ORATIO: PRAY

intercession & worship

KEYSTONE

Just as you received Christ Jesus the Lord, so continue to walk in Him, rooted and built up in Him and established in the faith, just as you were taught, abounding in thanksgiving. (ESV)

As ye have therefore received Christ Jesus the Lord, so walk ye in Him: Rooted and built up in Him, and stablished in the faith, as ye have been taught, abounding therein with thanksgiving.(KJV)

Colossians 2:6-7

RESPOND

CONTEMPLATIO: LIVE   *application & integration*

EVANGELII: GOSPEL   *contextualization & grace*

MEMORIA: MEMORIZE   *enscripturate & engrain*

COLOSSIANS 3

With the charity of Christ's Spirit give me to be rich in the wisdom of Christ's word; and let mine, O God, be a joyful Christianity, which effuses itself in glad and grateful acknowledgements that might be heard by the others to their instruction and encouragement in the ways of the divine life. Unseal my lips, O God; give me to be more open and pronounced in my testimony; put grace into my heart, to the overthrow of all that is good and gracious in my conduct.

Thomas Chalmers

REFLECT

LECTIO: READ

observation & knowledge

MEDITATIO: THINK

interpretation & discernment

ORATIO: PRAY

intercession & worship

KEYSTONE

Let the word of Christ dwell in you richly, teaching and admonishing one another in all wisdom, singing psalms and hymns and spiritual songs, with thankfulness in your hearts to God. (ESV)

Let the word of Christ dwell in you richly in all wisdom; teaching and admonishing one another in psalms and hymns and spiritual songs, singing with grace in your hearts to the Lord. (KJV)

Colossians 3:16

RESPOND

CONTEMPLATIO: LIVE   *application & integration*

EVANGELII: GOSPEL   *contextualization & grace*

MEMORIA: MEMORIZE   *enscripturate & engrain*

COLOSSIANS 4

Pour on me, O God, the spirit of grace and supplication; and may I watch as well as pray with all perserverance, mixing my grateful acknowledgments with my devout and unceasing supplications to the great Parent and Preserver of Men.

Thomas Chalmers

REFLECT

LECTIO: READ

observation & knowledge

MEDITATIO: THINK

interpretation & discernment

ORATIO: PRAY

intercession & worship

Walk in wisdom toward outsiders, making the best use of the time. Let your speech always be gracious, seasoned with salt, so that you may know how you ought to answer each person. (ESV)

Walk in wisdom toward them that are without, redeeming the time. Let your speech be always with grace, seasoned with salt, that ye may know how ye ought to answer every man. (KJV)

Colossians 4:5-6

RESPOND

CONTEMPLATIO: LIVE
application & integration

EVANGELII: GOSPEL
contextualization & grace

MEMORIA: MEMORIZE
enscripturate & engrain

I THESSALONIANS 1

He who hath delivered us from the wrath that is to come will accomplish for us another great and glorious deliverance, even from the corruption which still cleaves to us, and will continue so to do while we live in the present evil world (Galatians 1:4). Let me never forget the co-ordinate importance of these two deliverances. Doubtless He gave Himself for us to deliver us from the present evil world.

Thomas Chalmers

REFLECT

LECTIO: READ

observation & knowledge

MEDITATIO: THINK

interpretation & discernment

ORATIO: PRAY

intercession & worship

Our gospel came to you not only in word, but also in power and in the Holy Spirit and with full conviction. (ESV)

For our gospel came not unto you in word only, but also in power, and in the Holy Ghost, and in much assurance; as ye know what manner of men we were among you for your sake. (KJV)

I Thessalonians 1:5

RESPOND

CONTEMPLATIO: LIVE   *application & integration*

EVANGELII: GOSPEL   *contextualization & grace*

MEMORIA: MEMORIZE   *enscripturate & engrain*

1 THESSALONIANS 2

O may Thy word, Almighty Father, be received by us in faith, and work is us effectually. To this faith may we add virtue- fortitude- such a readiness as the Thessalonians had to brave all the persecution to which we might even in these times be exposed for our testimony to the truth as it is in Jesus.

Thomas Chalmers

REFLECT

LECTIO: READ

observation & knowledge

MEDITATIO: THINK

interpretation & discernment

ORATIO: PRAY

intercession & worship

KEYSTONE

Walk in a manner worthy of God, who calls you into His own kingdom and glory. (ESV)

That ye would walk worthy of God, who hath called you unto His kingdom and glory. (KJV)

I Thessalonians 2:12b

RESPOND

CONTEMPLATIO: LIVE
application & integration

EVANGELII: GOSPEL
contextualization & grace

MEMORIA: MEMORIZE
enscripturate & engrain

I THESSALONIANS 3

Thy will, O God, be done. Whatever the outward tribulations might be, let me inwardly grow in faith, and charity, and more especially, in love to the brethren, or affection for all good men. May this great central and presiding grace grow in me exceedingly, and may all the dependent and derived graces grow in me proportionally along with it.

Thomas Chalmers

REFLECT

LECTIO: READ
observation & knowledge

MEDITATIO: THINK
interpretation & discernment

ORATIO: PRAY
intercession & worship

KEYSTONE

May the Lord make you increase and abound in love for one another and for all. (ESV)

And the Lord make you to increase and abound in love one toward another, and toward all men. (KJV)

I Thessalonians 3:12

RESPOND

CONTEMPLATIO: LIVE   *application & integration*

EVANGELII: GOSPEL   *contextualization & grace*

MEMORIA: MEMORIZE   *enscripturate & engrain*

Let us not slight or despise that grace of inward chastity which is the office of the Spirit to work into our souls;- indeed the very essence Christian virtue seems to be holy love, love one to another, with a pure heart and fervently. He who loveth not knoweth not God, neither has been taught by Him.

Thomas Chalmers

REFLECT

LECTIO: READ

observation & knowledge

MEDITATIO: THINK

interpretation & discernment

ORATIO: PRAY

intercession & worship

KEYSTONE

God has not called us for impurity, but in holiness. (ESV)

For God hath not called us unto uncleanness, but unto holiness. (KJV)

I Thessalonians 4:7

RESPOND

CONTEMPLATIO: LIVE   *application & integration*

EVANGELII: GOSPEL   *contextualization & grace*

MEMORIA: MEMORIZE   *enscripturate & engrain*

I THESSALONIANS 5

I would joy in the Lord, and may that joy be my strength. I would joy in the Lord, and may that joy be my strength. I would pray with a constant aspiring and upward tendency towards God. And under every visitation, whether prosperous or adverse, I would that gratitude should always predominate, and have the victory in every trail or change of circumstances.

Thomas Chalmers

REFLECT

LECTIO: READ

observation & knowledge

MEDITATIO: THINK

interpretation & discernment

ORATIO: PRAY

intercession & worship

May the God of peace Himself sanctify you completely, and may your whole spirit and soul and body be kept blameless at the coming of our Lord Jesus Christ. He who calls you is faithful; He will surely do it. (ESV)

And the very God of peace sanctify you wholly; and I pray God your whole spirit and soul and body be preserved blameless unto the coming of our Lord Jesus Christ. Faithful is He that calleth you, who also will do it. (KJV)

I Thessalonians 5:23-24

RESPOND

CONTEMPLATIO: LIVE   *application & integration*

EVANGELII: GOSPEL   *contextualization & grace*

MEMORIA: MEMORIZE   *enscripturate & engrain*

II THESSALONIANS 1

Can I be said to adorn Christ's doctrine, though called to adorn it in all things? Can I be counted to walk worthy of this calling? God hath called me from uncleanness unto holiness, do I walk worthy of such a calling? Does my light so shine before men that in me, or in my good works, men are led to glorify God here? Thus and thus alone can the name of the Lord Jesus Christ be glorified in me and I in Him- an effect that can only result from the operation of the grace of our God and the Lord Jesus Christ upon me.

Thomas Chalmers

REFLECT

LECTIO: READ
observation & knowledge

MEDITATIO: THINK
interpretation & discernment

ORATIO: PRAY
intercession & worship

KEYSTONE

May the name of our Lord Jesus be glorified in you, and you in Him, according to the grace of our God and the Lord Jesus Christ. (ESV)

That the name of our Lord Jesus Christ may be glorified in you, and ye in Him, according to the grace of our God and the Lord Jesus Christ. (KJV)

II Thessalonians 1:12

RESPOND

CONTEMPLATIO: LIVE   *application & integration*

EVANGELII: GOSPEL   *contextualization & grace*

MEMORIA: MEMORIZE   *enscripturate & engrain*

II THESSALONIANS 2

One day is to the Lord as a thousand years, and a thousand years as one day. We are apt to magnify the present, its symptoms and prognostications, and yet what we now regard as immediate may, in the counsels of Him who maketh not haste, have to wait the evolutions of centuries. In His light we shall clearly see light.

Thomas Chalmers

REFLECT

LECTIO: READ

observation & knowledge

MEDITATIO: THINK

interpretation & discernment

ORATIO: PRAY

intercession & worship

KEYSTONE

Brothers, stand firm and hold to the traditions that you were taught by us, either by our spoken word or by our letter. (ESV)

Brethren, stand fast, and hold the traditions which ye have been taught, whether by word, or our epistle. (KJV)

II Thessalonians 2:15

RESPOND

CONTEMPLATIO: LIVE   *application & integration*

EVANGELII: GOSPEL   *contextualization & grace*

MEMORIA: MEMORIZE   *enscripturate & engrain*

II THESSALONIANS 3

The word of God does not suffice for the conversion of men but through the Spirit of God; and therefore to the preaching of the minister there should be superadded the prayers both of the minister and people.

Thomas Chalmers

REFLECT

LECTIO: READ

observation & knowledge

MEDITATIO: THINK

interpretation & discernment

ORATIO: PRAY

intercession & worship

KEYSTONE

Brothers, do not grow weary in doing good. (ESV)

But ye, brethren, be not weary in well doing. (KJV)

II Thessalonians 3:13

RESPOND

CONTEMPLATIO: LIVE   *application & integration*

EVANGELII: GOSPEL   *contextualization & grace*

MEMORIA: MEMORIZE   *enscripturate & engrain*

I TIMOTHY 1

The efficacious teaching of the sound gospel will powerfully and persuasively discipline me from all wickedness. But to make this reformation good, let me have the faith and the love which is in Christ Jesus. Let me receive it as a faithful saying and worthy of all acceptation- that He came into the world to save sinners. Blessed words!

Thomas Chalmers

REFLECT

LECTIO: READ

observation & knowledge

MEDITATIO: THINK

interpretation & discernment

ORATIO: PRAY

intercession & worship

KEYSTONE

The saying is trustworthy and deserving of full acceptance, that Christ Jesus came into the world to save sinners, of whom I am the foremost. (ESV)

This is a faithful saying, and worthy of all acceptation, that Christ Jesus came into the world to save sinners; of whom I am chief. (KJV)

I Timothy 1:15

RESPOND

CONTEMPLATIO: LIVE   *application & integration*

EVANGELII: GOSPEL   *contextualization & grace*

MEMORIA: MEMORIZE   *enscripturate & engrain*

I TIMOTHY 2

Let us ask both for ourselves and others till we receive, let us seek till we find, let us knock till the door be opened to us. Let us keep by the plain duty enjoied upon us-pray everywhere and for every creature, in the spirit of faith towards God, and of forgiveness towards all men. Thus shall we pray without wrath and without doubting.

Thomas Chalmers

REFLECT

LECTIO: READ

observation & knowledge

MEDITATIO: THINK

interpretation & discernment

ORATIO: PRAY

intercession & worship

There is one God, and there is one mediator between God and men, the man Christ Jesus. (ESV)

For there is one God, and one mediator between God and men, the man Christ Jesus. (KJV)

I Timothy 2:5

RESPOND

CONTEMPLATIO: LIVE
application & integration

EVANGELII: GOSPEL
contextualization & grace

MEMORIA: MEMORIZE
enscripturate & engrain

How instructive is the value annexed to general reputation; and we further meet with the repetition of a former testimony to the alliance which obtains between faith and a good conscience. We conceive it to another trait of the preternatural sagacity of the Bible.

Thomas Chalmers

REFLECT

LECTIO: READ

observation & knowledge

MEDITATIO: THINK

interpretation & discernment

ORATIO: PRAY

intercession & worship

KEYSTONE

You may know how one ought to behave in the household of God, which is the church of the living God, a pillar and buttress of the truth. (ESV)

Thou mayest know how thou oughtest to behave thyself in the house of God, which is the church of the living God, the pillar and ground of the truth. (KJV)

I Timothy 3:15

RESPOND

CONTEMPLATIO: LIVE   *application & integration*

EVANGELII: GOSPEL   *contextualization & grace*

MEMORIA: MEMORIZE   *enscripturate & engrain*

I TIMOTHY 4

Let me mix up with all my enjoyments a grateful sense of Thee as the Giver; but let me mix up with every gratification both prayer and the ministry of the word- so that when using the world I may not abuse it. May I be stablished in the faith and exercised unto godliness.

Thomas Chalmers

REFLECT

LECTIO: READ

observation & knowledge

MEDITATIO: THINK

interpretation & discernment

ORATIO: PRAY

intercession & worship

Keep a close watch on yourself and on the teaching. Persist in this, for by so doing you will save both yourself and your hearers. (ESV)

Take heed unto thyself, and unto the doctrine; continue in them: for in doing this thou shalt both save thyself, and them that hear thee. (KJV)

I Timothy 4:16

RESPOND

CONTEMPLATIO: LIVE   *application & integration*

EVANGELII: GOSPEL   *contextualization & grace*

MEMORIA: MEMORIZE   *enscripturate & engrain*

I TIMOTHY 5

Enable me to rebuke both in wisdom and in charity, and, moreover, with all purity. What a pertinency and wisdom shine forth even in the minute clauses of Scripture! Give me, O Lord, the requisite boldness, but save me from partiality.

Thomas Chalmers

REFLECT

LECTIO: READ   *observation & knowledge*

MEDITATIO: THINK   *interpretation & discernment*

ORATIO: PRAY   *intercession & worship*

Do not be hasty in the laying on of hands, nor take part in the sins of others; keep yourself pure. (ESV)

Lay hands suddenly on no man, neither be partaker of other men's sins: keep thyself pure. (KJV)

I Timothy 5:22

RESPOND

CONTEMPLATIO: LIVE
application & integration

EVANGELII: GOSPEL
contextualization & grace

MEMORIA: MEMORIZE
enscripturate & engrain

1 TIMOTHY 6

O my God, conform me in all respects to that doctrine which is according to godliness. Give me to understand that the wholesome doctrine of our Gospel comprehends more than the mere dogmata of our faith- in the treatment of which we may do little better than dote about questions and idle logomachies. Such a practical habitude will be my best preservation against errors concerning the faith, and thus shall I avoid the babblings or vain controversy.

Thomas Chalmers

REFLECT

LECTIO: READ

observation & knowledge

MEDITATIO: THINK

interpretation & discernment

ORATIO: PRAY

intercession & worship

KEYSTONE

Pursue righteousness, godliness, faith, love, steadfastness, and gentleness. (ESV)

Follow after righteousness, godliness, faith, love, patience, meekness. (KJV)

I Timothy 6:11

RESPOND

CONTEMPLATIO: LIVE

application & integration

EVANGELII: GOSPEL

contextualization & grace

MEMORIA: MEMORIZE

enscripturate & engrain

II TIMOTHY 1

The Gospel of Jesus Christ is the promise of life through Him. And therefore would I pray with all confidence for the grace that sanctifies, the mercy that pardons, the peace that allays all my disquietudes; and let me maintain that pure conscience- that conscience void of offence, without which faith will be shipwrecked.

Thomas Chalmers

REFLECT

LECTIO: READ

observation & knowledge

MEDITATIO: THINK

interpretation & discernment

ORATIO: PRAY

intercession & worship

I am not ashamed, for I know whom I have believed, and I am convinced that He is able to guard until that Day what has been entrusted to me. (ESV)

I am not ashamed: for I know whom I have believed, and am persuaded that He is able to keep that which I have committed unto him against that day. (KJV)

II Timothy 1:12b

RESPOND

CONTEMPLATIO: LIVE

application & integration

EVANGELII: GOSPEL

contextualization & grace

MEMORIA: MEMORIZE

enscripturate & engrain

II TIMOTHY 2

Give me the wisdom of rightly dividing the word of truth, one part of it from another; and also of rightly distributing to each a word in season, making a study of its varied adaptations to the varieties of human experience. Let me refrain from idle and unnecessary questions, often leading to dangerous heresies; and may I hold it enough to be sound in the weightier matters both of the Christian faith and the Christian practice.

Thomas Chalmers

REFLECT

LECTIO: READ

observation & knowledge

MEDITATIO: THINK

interpretation & discernment

ORATIO: PRAY

intercession & worship

KEYSTONE

The saying is trustworthy, for: if we have died with Him, we will also live with Him; if we endure, we will also reign with Him; if we deny Him, He also will deny us; if we are faithless, He remains faithful—for He cannot deny Himself. (ESV)

It is a faithful saying: For if we be dead with Him, we shall also live with Him: If we suffer, we shall also reign with Him: if we deny Him, He also will deny us: If we believe not, yet He abideth faithful: He cannot deny Himself. (KJV)

II Timothy 2:11-13

RESPOND

CONTEMPLATIO: LIVE   *application & integration*

EVANGELII: GOSPEL   *contextualization & grace*

MEMORIA: MEMORIZE   *enscripturate & engrain*

II TIMOTHY 3

O by means of the blessed Scriptures may I become wise unto salvation. What a blessing to know that all Scripture is given by inspiration from God, and that all is profitable. What a practical thing out and out is Christianity!

Thomas Chalmers

REFLECT

LECTIO: READ

observation & knowledge

MEDITATIO: THINK

interpretation & discernment

ORATIO: PRAY

intercession & worship

KEYSTONE

All Scripture is breathed out by God and profitable for teaching, for reproof, for correction, and for training in righteousness, that the man of God may be complete, equipped for every good work. (ESV)

All scripture is given by inspiration of God, and is profitable for doctrine, for reproof, for correction, for instruction in righteousness: That the man of God may be perfect, thoroughly furnished unto all good works. (KJV)

II Timothy 3:16-17

RESPOND

CONTEMPLATIO: LIVE   *application & integration*

EVANGELII: GOSPEL   *contextualization & grace*

MEMORIA: MEMORIZE   *enscripturate & engrain*

II TIMOTHY 4

There is a spurious, and I fear a fashionable orthodoxy, regulated by the cadence of the form of sound words, but adverse to the sound doctrine which is according to the godliness, and which teaches men to live aright as well as to think aright.

Thomas Chalmers

REFLECT

LECTIO: READ
observation & knowledge

MEDITATIO: THINK
interpretation & discernment

ORATIO: PRAY
intercession & worship

KEYSTONE

Preach the word; be ready in season and out of season; reprove, rebuke, and exhort, with complete patience and teaching. (ESV)

Preach the word; be instant in season, out of season; reprove, rebuke, exhort with all long suffering and doctrine. (KJV)

II Timothy 4:2

RESPOND

CONTEMPLATIO: LIVE   *application & integration*

EVANGELII: GOSPEL   *contextualization & grace*

MEMORIA: MEMORIZE   *enscripturate & engrain*

TITUS 1

O my God, let me at length be practically and powerfully impressed by the repeated testimonies and demands of Thy word on behalf of purity. Purify my heart by faith.

Thomas Chalmers

REFLECT

LECTIO: READ

observation & knowledge

MEDITATIO: THINK

interpretation & discernment

ORATIO: PRAY

intercession & worship

KEYSTONE

An overseer, as God's steward, must be above reproach. (ESV)

For a bishop must be blameless, as the steward of God. (KJV)

Titus 1:7

------------ RESPOND ------------

CONTEMPLATIO: LIVE

application & integration

EVANGELII: GOSPEL

contextualization & grace

MEMORIA: MEMORIZE

enscripturate & engrain

TITUS 2

Our habitual attitude should be that of looking unto Jesus. He gave Himself for us, no doubt, to expiate our sins, but the ulterior, the terminating purpose, was to turn us from sin unto righteousness. He died to redeem us from guilt, but this with a view to something beyond, even to our personal sanctification, and that we should become zealous of good works. Let me henceforth serve, not in the oldness of the letter, but in the newness of the Spirit.

Thomas Chalmers

REFLECT

LECTIO: READ

observation & knowledge

MEDITATIO: THINK

interpretation & discernment

ORATIO: PRAY

intercession & worship

KEYSTONE

The grace of God has appeared, bringing salvation for all people, training us to renounce ungodliness and worldly passions, and to live self-controlled, upright, and godly lives in the present age, waiting for our blessed hope, the appearing of the glory of our great God and Savior Jesus Christ, who gave Himself for us to redeem us from all lawlessness and to purify for Himself a people for His own possession who are zealous for good works. (ESV)

For the grace of God that bringeth salvation hath appeared to all men, teaching us that, denying ungodliness and worldly lusts, we should live soberly, righteously, and godly, in this present world; Looking for that blessed hope, and the glorious appearing of the great God and our Saviour Jesus Christ; Who gave himself for us, that He might redeem us from all iniquity, and purify unto Himself a peculiar people, zealous of good works. (KJV)

Titus 2:11-14

RESPOND

CONTEMPLATIO: LIVE   *application & integration*

EVANGELII: GOSPEL   *contextualization & grace*

MEMORIA: MEMORIZE   *enscripturate & engrain*

TITUS 3

And let me ever keep fast hold of the precious truth that by grae I am justified, and that not by my own works of righteousness, but by the love, and kindness, and mercy of God I am saved. It is only thus indeed that I am a rightful heir of the blissful immortality in heaven. Let all this be affirmed constantly, in order that they who believe should be careful to maintain good works, both for what is a necessary and what is profitable, avoiding, on the other hand, those vain controversies which are unprofitable.

Thomas Chalmers

REFLECT

LECTIO: READ

observation & knowledge

MEDITATIO: THINK

interpretation & discernment

ORATIO: PRAY

intercession & worship

KEYSTONE

When the goodness and loving kindness of God our Savior appeared, He saved us, not because of works done by us in righteousness, but according to His own mercy, by the washing of regeneration and renewal of the Holy Spirit. (ESV)

But after that the kindness and love of God our Saviour toward man appeared, not by works of righteousness which we have done, but according to His mercy He saved us, by the washing of regeneration, and renewing of the Holy Ghost. (KJV)

Titus 3:4-5

RESPOND

CONTEMPLATIO: LIVE
application & integration

EVANGELII: GOSPEL
contextualization & grace

MEMORIA: MEMORIZE
enscripturate & engrain

PHILEMON 1

Let us learn that the most effectual method of communicating our faith to others is to make it palpable or known to them that, because in Christ, we abound in all good works and graces.

Thomas Chalmers

REFLECT

LECTIO: READ

observation & knowledge

MEDITATIO: THINK

interpretation & discernment

ORATIO: PRAY

intercession & worship

I pray that the sharing of your faith may become effective for the full knowledge of every good thing that is in us for the sake of Christ. (ESV)

That the communication of thy faith may become effectual by the acknowledging of every good thing which is in you in Christ Jesus. (KJV)

Philemon 1:6

RESPOND

CONTEMPLATIO: LIVE   *application & integration*

EVANGELII: GOSPEL   *contextualization & grace*

MEMORIA: MEMORIZE   *enscripturate & engrain*

AFTERWORD:
READING CHALMERS TODAY

"Let me not be content either with a zeal without knowledge, or a knowledge without zeal. May Thy grace open a way for Thy Word to our hearts, and strengthen us to act upon it."

Thomas Chalmers

"There is not, of course, any difficulty in explaining the indifference of the modern secular mind to Chalmers, neither is it surprising that churchmen of liberal persuasion should lack enthusiasm for his memory. What is more problematical is the question why Evangelical and Reformed Christianity should have made so little of him these many years."

Iain Murray

"It was not so much his words, as the virtue that went out of him, that turned our hearts toward the heathen. Dr. Chalmers made us see the world—and then, what might be possible in it."

W.S. MacKay

I am often asked how to begin a serious study of the life and work of Thomas Chalmers. This is at least partly because I can hardly ever give a lecture, preach a sermon, write an essay, or post a blog without mentioning him. But even more, it is because reading Chalmers can prove to be an arduous and elusive pursuit.

Don't be fooled by the fact that at the beginning of the nineteenth century, Chalmers was heralded as the greatest preacher in the English-speaking world: he is very difficult to read. His vocabulary was vast, his Scots syntax is peculiar to those of us accustomed to the less circuitous English spoken south of the Tweed, and his pre-Victorian, Regency era rhetorical formalism is quite alien to modern readers and speakers of the King's Tongue. Plowing through his dense style is more than a little difficult—but it is also very much worth the effort.

It is worth the effort, that is, if you can find his works to plow through. And that is no easy matter either. Virtually all of his books have long been out of print. Reprints are not only few and far between, they tend to be scanned from antiquarian library copies rather than newly, clearly typeset. You can find quite an array of titles in the Google Books and Guttenberg Project digital collections—but they lack the context that good introductory essays, explanatory footnotes and historical references, and deep indexing might provide.

The first book to which I always send readers is the short profile by John Roxborough and Stuart Piggen entitled, *The St. Andrew Seven* (Banner of Truth). Though not entirely about Chalmers (most of the text is devoted to six of his students and the way he influenced the trajectory of their lives and ministries) it is nevertheless the best single, accessible work available in a modern edition.

The doctoral thesis of John Roxborogh is likewise very helpful. *Thomas Chalmers: Enthusiast For Mission* (Rutherford House and Paternoster Press) is a concise examination of the parish vision and missional structure Chalmers helped to institutionalize in the Free Kirk.

In terms of biography, the most helpful work currently in print is a single chapter in Iain Murray's *A Scottish Christian Heritage* (Banner of Truth). As he always seems to be able to do, Murray captures the heart and soul of both the Gospel message and the human, historical means by which that message is proclaimed in this poor fallen world.

Another helpful doctoral dissertation recently published, but alas now out of print, is Stephen Brown's *Thomas Chalmers and the Godly Commonwealth* (Oxford). Serving as a critical biography, the work affords useful balance to the historical and theological reader.

Of the nearly one hundred works actually written by Chalmers, only the two volumes of his *Sabbath Scripture Readings* (Solid Ground) and his *Letters* (Banner of Truth) remain in print. The *Readings* are delightful *Lectio Divina* meditations on individual chapters of Scripture written for his personal devotions during the last few years of his life. They provide us with a remarkable glimpse into both his heart and his ministry, his piety and his hermeneutic. In addition, the quotations used in Keystones are taken from these *Sabbath Readings*. The *Letters* portray the great man at work, at home, on the stump, in the midst of controversy, in the classroom, and amongst his brethren in a way that only a collection of personal correspondence possibly could.

Of his sermons, only *The Expulsive Power of a New Affection* is widely available—including as a beautifully typeset PDF on GeorgeGrant.net. It is genius and certainly warrants the attentions of serious students of the Gospel. But a host of his other works are as valuable. A new, annotated edition of his most accessible works should be a high priority for an enterprising publisher—as would a new comprehensive biography and in-depth studies of his parish vision, missional strategies, and church planting endeavors.

I have long thought that something like what James Bratt has undertaken to rehabilitate the life and work of Abraham Kuyper, needs to be done for the life and work of Chalmers. But until someone is able to take up that substantial mantle, we will have to content ourselves with a handful of scattered resources (I am presently working on several projects, including a full biography, *A Wider Diameter of Light*, an anthology of his sermons and lectures, quotes and epigrams, *The Expulsive Power*, and an analysis of the parish system he recovered, *Parish Life*, in addition to the three volumes of his Keystones discipleship and Bible memory system).

Chalmers once asserted, "No matter how large, your vision is too small." My own vision for recovering the work of Chalmers from undue obscurity is large, but I am quite certain that in this too, he is right: it remains too small.

GEORGE GRANT

George Grant is the Pastor of Parish Presbyterian Church, Director of the King's Meadow Study Center, Founder of Franklin Classical School, Bannockburn College, and New College Franklin, and serves as the Coordinator of the Chalmers Fund. He is the author of dozens of books in the areas of history, biography, politics, literature, and social criticism and he has written hundreds of essays, articles, and columns. His work on behalf of the homeless, for international relief and development, for racial reconciliation, and for the sanctity of life has been widely profiled, though he is probably best known for his pioneering efforts to establish Classical Christian Schools in the US and around the world. His books, podcasts, curricula, sermons, and lectures are available at www.ParishPres.org and www.GeorgeGrant.net. He makes his home in Middle Tennessee near the historic town of Franklin with his wife and co-author Karen. Together they have three grown children and six grandchildren.

THOMAS CHALMERS

Thomas Chalmers (1780-1847) was a Scottish pastor, professor, author, political economist, and social reformer. He was a pioneer of church planting, Bible societies, and overseas missions efforts during the tumultuous days following the Napoleonic Wars. The author of dozens of bestselling books, he was widely heralded as one of the greatest preachers and orators of the day. He led the Evangelical party through the Disruption of the Church of Scotland and afterward helped to establish the Free Church—with more than five hundred new congregations in the span of just five years. But he is perhaps best known for the discipling impact he had on the young men he taught at the University of St. Andrews, the University of Edinburgh, and New College Edinburgh. During the last twenty years of his life, he lived at Church Hill in the Morningside neighborhood southwest of Edinburgh with his wife Grace and their six daughters.

KEYSTONES

MAKE DISCIPLES

Standfast Books
Franklin, Tennessee

Made in the USA
Lexington, KY
25 November 2019